What If My Cat . . . ?

fights with other cats . . . doesn't use the litter box . . . scratches the furniture . . . kills birds . . . has mad moments . . . etc . . . etc?

Expert answers to all those catty problems

Claire Arrowsmith and Francesa Riccomini

BARRON'S

First edition for the United States and Canada published in 2008 by Barron's Educational Series, Inc.

First published in 2008 by Interpet Publishing

All inquiries should be addressed to:
Barron's Educational Series, Inc.
250 Wireless Boulevard
Hauppauge, NY 11788
www.barronseduc.com

ISBN-13: 978-0-7641-3903-1
ISBN-10: 0-7641-3903-7

Library of Congress Control Number: 2007926216

Printed and bound in China

9 8 7 6 5 4 3 2 1

The methods described in this book are kind and fair to the animal, but owners must understand that each case merits individual assessment. To ensure the welfare of your cat, you should discuss your concerns with your veterinarian and a qualified animal behaviorist, especially where illness, aggression, or extreme anxiety are involved. For the purposes of easy reading, cats are described as "he" throughout this book unless the topic specifically relates to female cats. This by no means infers any preference, nor should it be taken as an indication that either sex is particularly problematic.

Acknowledgments

My sincere gratitude goes out to all those people who have helped and supported me while I wrote this book. Firstly, thanks must go to the editorial and production team, who helped to create the idea and form my words into the final product. Thank you for this opportunity.
I would like to acknowledge the help of my teachers and the behaviorists who have influenced and encouraged me and who have shown me that there's always so much more to learn in this field.
My thanks go to my family, who offer support in so many ways, and all my friends who were patient enough to read various drafts and convert my "Claire-isms" into regular English.
The final mention goes to my husband, who has provided his unending support and patience during my ventures as an animal behaviorist. You always believe in me; thank you.

Dedication:
Sooty.
A more tolerant, patient cat I have yet to meet.

About the Authors

Claire Arrowsmith was raised in the Highlands of Scotland with a range of domestic, farm and wild animals, which fueled her love of and interest in all animals, particularly cats and dogs. Claire is a full member of the Association of Pet Behaviour Counsellors (APBC) and runs her own behavioral consultancy. She holds an Honours degree in Zoology and a Masters degree in Applied Animal Behavior and Animal Welfare. Claire has worked in animal rescue and with Hearing Dogs for Deaf People. She is also the specialist behaviorist for Houndstar Films DVDs, who produce cat, dog, and small animal advisory DVDs. Claire writes for *Your Dog* magazine, providing expert answers to reader's questions, and presents regular advisory talks and workshops about problem pets. She currently lives with her husband and Rhodesian Ridgeback mix dog, Sarnie.

Francesca Riccomini BSc(Hons) BVetMed MRCVS DipAS(CABC) CCAB graduated from the Royal Veterinary College, University of London, and spent many years as a small animal veterinarian before gaining a Post-Graduate Diploma in Companion Animal Behaviour Counselling from Southampton University and specializing in behavioral medicine.

She is a Certified Clinical Animal Behaviorist, a member of the Feline Advisory Bureau's (FAB) Expert Behaviour Panel, and a full member of the Association of Pet Behaviour Counsellors (APBC), for which she formerly served as Veterinary Representative.

Francesca is a co-author of the FAB's first book dedicated to the *Cat Friendly Practice*, and the recently published *Essential Cattitude, An Insight into the Feline World*. In addition, she writes companion animal behavior-related articles for a number of publications, including several veterinary titles and magazines aimed at pet owners. She also addresses readers' behavioral queries for *Your Cat* magazine.

A regular speaker at seminars and conferences, an aspect of her behavioral practice that Francesca finds particularly rewarding, she firmly believes that companion animal behavior, and problems relating to it, is of paramount importance in both the veterinary and pet-owning worlds.

Over the years numerous "rescued" cats and dogs have enriched Francesca's life, although she is currently between pets, and, while enjoying the freedom that accompanies a pet-free status, she is greatly looking forward to the next animal companion that comes along.

CONTENTS

PART 2

HABITS AND MISHAPS AROUND THE HOME Pages 38–71

What if my cat . . .

PART

3

MISHAPS AND PROBLEMS DURING SOCIAL INTERACTIONS Pages 72–97

What if my cat . . .

PART

6

THE AGING CAT: Pages 150–153

What if my cat . . .

Introduction

This book is intended to help improve the lives of both owners and the cats in their care. Understanding the history and behavioral development of your cat will help you to discover what makes him tick. This should help you to improve your skills as a cat owner and allow you to recognize and manage any mishaps. It will hopefully allow you to understand what your cat needs to live an enriched and fulfilled life. Whether your cat has been lucky to have had a stable and loving home since kittenhood, or whether you have opened your home to a stray or a rescue cat, I hope that the information in this book will help you to live alongside him as peacefully and amicably as possible.

The book is comprised of six chapters which deal with: understanding your cat and his history and development; possible issues within the home; social interaction difficulties; problems outdoors and in new places; preventing and coping with illness; and, finally, the aging cat. The chapters are structured around a series of "What ifs . . . ?" that allow you to easily access the information relevant to your current problem or query. The topics are linked and cross-referenced, which enables you to seek out further details related to your question or topic of interest. You will find explanations about why your cat performs a particular behavior or why a problem may have arisen and then receive guidance on how to overcome each issue. You will also read about **how to prevent problems** from occurring, because avoiding the development of inappropriate behaviors is always the ideal solution.

I hope that the information in this book proves of some benefit for every reader, either through being a source of interesting information or by helping you to manage and control a specific problem. I also hope that the cats sharing your home can live a better and more fulfilled life and that we humans can all continue to enjoy sharing our lives with a full appreciation of the qualities of our feline friends.

Claire Arrowsmith

UNDERSTANDING YOUR CAT—HIS ROLE AS A PET, HIS HISTORY, AND HIS DEVELOPMENT

PART

1

WHAT IFs . . . ?

What if my cat . . .

OWNING A CAT

Below: Cats are not as unsociable as often thought, and they can share wonderful, warm relationships with their human companions.

Normally, owning a cat brings the pleasure of companionship and the benefits of living with a pet. On first consideration, owning cats may seem like quite an easy option. You don't need to walk them or go to training classes, and they are small and easy to leave at home while you work. Their independent tendencies are attractive to those of us who have demanding work schedules and family lives.

There are numerous benefits that come from owning a cat. Petting a happy cat benefits the owner by lowering blood pressure and promoting a feeling of relaxation. Pet cats provide company for the elderly or housebound, who would otherwise spend long periods alone. There is also evidence that people live longer if they own pets for extended periods during their lives.

However, sometimes things do go wrong, and the cat-owner relationship can become strained. Owners of any animal must understand what a *normal* or *abnormal* behavior for that species is. This will allow you to recognize signals from your pet that help you to identify or prevent problems, both medical and behavioral. *Cats are very different from humans* and so we must *not* try to implement methods just because they make sense when applied to our own human health issues, child-caring routines, or our relationships.

OVERCOMING PROBLEMS IN CATS

Living with cats can be extremely rewarding, but when problems do occur, the benefits of cat ownership can seem insignificant compared to the damage or inconvenience caused. Problems often result from a clash between normal feline instincts and the boundaries of behavior that we humans view as acceptable. Most problems actually stem from your cat

Far right: *Cats are often expected to adapt their own behavior to suit their owner's lifestyle.*

Below: *Regular health checks and advice from your veterinarian will help you to distinguish more clearly between medical and behavioral problems.*

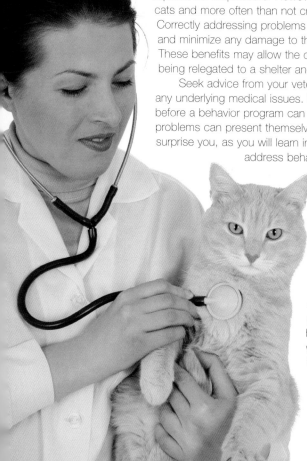

being unable to express his full feline instincts due to his current lifestyle.

Behavioral difficulties should be addressed as early as possible to maximize the chances for a successful outcome. Leaving problems to resolve themselves often results in increasingly complex situations and eventually the breakdown of the owner-cat relationship. This leads to the disturbing number of cats that are put down or re-homed every year.

Many behavioral issues in cats stem from anxiety and stress, so it's vital for the cat's well-being that he is helped as early as possible. Punishment is often one of the first responses used by owners, because it seems to be a logical way to express our displeasure. However, this is upsetting and confusing for cats and more often than not creates more problems than it solves. Correctly addressing problems early can help to avoid a lot of stress and minimize any damage to the home and consequent expense. These benefits may allow the cat to remain in your home rather than being relegated to a shelter and so ultimately may save his life.

Seek advice from your veterinarian, who will check your cat for any underlying medical issues. It's absolutely vital to address any illness before a behavior program can be embarked upon. Feline health problems can present themselves in an array of symptoms that may surprise you, as you will learn in Part 5. It's unfair and unhelpful to address behavior problems in a sick cat. When your vet has ruled out medical issues, he or she will refer you to a recommended animal behaviorist with proper credentials.

What if my cat . . . ? addresses the most common problems noted by owners and behaviorists. Patience and understanding will be required when tackling any problem, but the companionship of your cat and the pleasure you experience living with a happy animal will make your commitment worthwhile. This book will also indicate to you **when you should seek expert help** from your veterinarian or qualified animal behaviorist, because some health or behavioral issues require urgent individual attention.

15

CHOOSING YOUR CAT

Cats are now the most commonly kept household pet. Choosing a new cat to join your family is an exciting time, and picking the correct companion is important. You will need to consider carefully what type of household you have—is it busy or quiet? Do you have young children or other pets? This should influence the type and character of the cat you choose. A timid, quiet cat would find it difficult to cope with boisterous children, grumpy cats, or exuberant dogs. Think about your home's suitability for a feline tenant **before** you embark on finding one. Be realistic and honest with yourself about how you feel about cat hair, cleaning litter boxes, and all the other things that accompany owning a cat. A cat's life expectancy is now roughly 16 years, and some live many years longer, so take time making your decision. A cat deserves a stable and caring home for life.

There are many places where you can acquire a new cat. Sadly, cat rescues are full of unwanted kittens and adults in need of suitable homes so it's worth beginning your search there. Every year thousands of cats require re-homing through rescues. Elderly and dark-colored cats find it particularly difficult to find new homes. Visit your local shelters and take your time viewing the cats to see if any seem suitable for your home. Remember that they will feel stressed in the shelter environment and may not show themselves off to their full potential, because a stressed cat is likely to sit quietly at the back of the pen. Once at home, this cat may express a great character. Don't let your heart rule your mind when it comes to making the final decision; it's unfair to take on a cat that does not suit your lifestyle.

If you are determined to get a kitten or a cat with a known history, then your vet or friends may also know of house-bred litter or adults that are in need of homes. It's not advisable to buy your cat from a pet shop or market stall, because you do not know about his health or the health and welfare of the mother, and you may not have adequate support should you have any questions or problems. Buying these animals only lines the pockets of the people producing them and guarantees another space that they will fill with another litter.

Plan ahead and make sure that you have made your home and yard secure, removed any dangerous items and plants (see Part 5, "What if?" No.139), and purchased food, bedding, grooming equipment, and toys. Find out where your local vets are and talk to them about vaccinations and a regular worming and flea program. Too many cats are not health-checked regularly and, as a result, often present at the vet with later stages of disease than dogs.

Above: Cats of all ages, colors, and characters find themselves living in rescue shelters while new homes are sought for them.

Pedigree Cats

If you have your heart set on a pedigree cat, then make sure that you research the breed so that you understand the typical behavior patterns and requirements. You will also need to be aware of health conditions that affec

Siamese

Black Domestic Shorthair

that breed so you can search for a healthy breeding line. If you cannot tolerate an active hunter or want a quiet house cat, then certain breeds will be less suitable than others. Visiting cat shows will allow you to encounter different breeds and talk to owners about their characters. Spend time researching breeders, and choose one with a good reputation. Don't be offended if a breeder asks you lots of questions about your household, routine, and previous cat experience. Good breeders will be keen to ensure their kittens go to perfect homes, and by vetting you in this way they are being responsible.

Does color matter? It may be easy to be swayed by the looks of a cat, but always put character and suitability as a pet first. Some myths about colors in cats can be confusing. It's true that coat color is thought to be linked to different character types, but there are no absolute rules, and it's more important to choose a well socialized, healthy cat. Tabby cats and tortoiseshell are versions of cat colors rather than actual breeds. Tortoiseshell cats are mostly females, but males do occur, though they are normally sterile. Although ginger cats are commonly male, ginger females can also arise. Don't be fooled into paying large amounts for either of these, because they are no more valuable than other domestic cats.

White cats with blue eyes are usually deaf, with the exception of Burmese and Siamese types. Pale cats can be more seriously affected by the sun than darker colors, so you will have to be aware and limit sun exposure or apply cat-friendly sun screen during summer months. Many superstitions and old-wives tales claim that black cats are lucky. Scientists have found that the black gene might be "lucky" in one way because it may be linked to a better defense against infections.

Whatever color of cat you choose, his feline instincts and desires will still be the same.

Left: *Different breeds come in a variety of colors, but unless you'll be showing your cat competitively, the personality is the most important feature to look for.*

FELINE ANCESTRY

Below: *Even the fanciest pedigree cat retains behavioral characteristics from his ancestors.*

Far right: *The species Felis sylvestris is wide-ranging and includes the African Wildcat (F. s. lybica), which appears to have been the group most adaptable to human domestication. Selection for color and "type" has resulted in the wide range of cats seen around the world today.*

Cats belong to the family Felidae. There are 37 species of cats in the wor today. They have adapted and evolved in all parts of the world except Antarctica, showing how highly versatile they are.

Early settlers encouraged small cats into their villages and camps to help control the vermin populations that plagued agricultural settlements. Once people recognized the benefits cats brought to their lives, they acti began to seek out kittens to keep in their homes. The cats gained from having a plentiful supply of food and shelter, and humans gained from disease prevention and companionship. This relationship has continued through the ages and has hardly changed until this day. The domestic cat in your living room shows remarkable similarities to its wild counterpart because we have only recently intervened by limiting reproduction through neutering or restricting access to the outdoors and, therefore, to possible mates. Prior to this, pet and feral cats regularly interbred, allowing the free flow of genes among the populations.

Archaeological evidence shows us cats were living alongside humans 9,500 years ago, and there is DNA evidence to suggest that house cats diverged from their larger ancestors as far back as 13,000 years ago. The precise origin of our domestic cat, *Felis silvestris catus*, has been mu debated, but recent DNA evidence indicates that they actually have a Nea Eastern origin. It is thought that the domestic cat's closest wild relation is the African Wildcat *(Felis silvestris lybica)*.

It helps to appreciate that your pet cat still bears striking similarities to his wild cousins. This knowledge can help you to build a healthy respect f him, his abilities, and his reactions.

CAT SOCIETY

Cats differ from dogs, who live in social groups and rely upon one anothe for hunting, protection, and ultimately survival. Cats evolved mainly as soli hunters and are much more adapted to living alone, hunting alone, and relying upon their own senses to keep them safe. They don't have to work groups, which makes it much harder to coerce them into following our rule To put it simply, a cat will stay within a group **if** he feels that he is getting something positive from the relationship. If not, he will simply choose not t

Right: The various types of small cat species have evolved to be perfect solitary hunters. They prey upon small animals that can easily be subdued without the help of a pack. Compared to humans, or even dogs, the behavior of cats may seem rather unsociable, though the truth is that cats simply have different social needs.

Below: Natural groups of cats often comprise several related females who may help to care for each other's kittens. This benefits the group by ensuring the kittens have a better chance of survival.

be involved. This is why the old-fashioned training techniques used to force our pet dogs to behave have no success with cats. It's not that the cat is in any way less intelligent, he simply has less desire to conform in order to be part of your pack. If he feels uncomfortable, then he'll resort to being solitary and self-reliant once more and may indicate his discomfort by spraying or another unwanted behavior.

The preference for solitary hunting and self-reliance does not mean that domestic cats are not sociable; they are simply social in a different way from us. The cat's complex society often confuses owners, because it's common to own several cats together. The truth is that cats have different social rules depending on what they are doing, how they have developed, and what their environment has to offer. Your cat may live with several others in your home, but these may not all belong to the same "social" group.

In a feral situation the males of reproductive age often roam alone or are involved in male gangs. Typically, only one breeding male is present in each group of females. **Related females** often live together in groups. They may help one another raise kittens, sharing cleaning and feeding roles. These natural group structures can help you plan your groups and understand social conflict.

CAT SENSES AND PHYSICAL DESIGN

All members of the feline family display incredible designs that make them perfect carnivores. Cats are able to control their movements precisely; this together with their amazingly adapted senses, makes them highly success predators. It's virtually impossible for a human to imagine how a cat perceives the world, because feline senses are so different from ours.

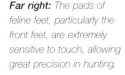

The **sense of smell** is critical and allows a cat to recognize territor boundaries, identify group members, determine the freshness of food items, and detect mates. The *ability to smell is vital* to cats, and we can see how important it is when we study individuals that have lost the smell due to viruses or other illness. These cats often lose their appetite their toileting habits change, and they are less likely to perform courtship behaviors. Some specialists describe cats as "living in clouds of scent" that act as sign posts, influencing emotions and replacing the need for some visual recognition.

Cat **eyesight** is developed for hunting. Cats are farsighted and probably rely more on the information from their whiskers and sce for the detection of close-up movement. They are very sensitive t fast, horizontal movements, which makes them fantastic at spotting the movement of prey. They have no need to detect a range of colors.

The **sense of touch** is also highly developed in the cat, especially in the nose and pads of the feet, allowing them to manipulate their prey well. This helps to make up for their sight being poorer at close range.

Feline hearing is acute and optimized to hear a different frequency range from that which humans experience. Cats can actually hear the same frequencies that small rodents use to communicate, making them perfect predators. Interestingly, cats are also tuned in to the range used by the human voice, so they have adapted well to life alongside people.

Far right: The pads of feline feet, particularly the front feet, are extremely sensitive to touch, allowing great precision in hunting.

Physical Abilities

The Tail Cats are renowned for their amazing sense of balance. They are able to process information very quickly and so can easily adjust their position as they prowl about their territory or play. Watch your cat and see how the tail moves to act as a counterweight.

The Whiskers Your cat's whiskers, or vibrissae, are extremely important because they provide information about the space around him, allowing accurate movement even in the dark. They are located in rows around the face and head, and some are even found on the backs of the front legs. T whiskers are critical to your cat's ability to judge spaces and are extremely sensitive because they are connected to many nerve endings. Under no circumstances should whiskers be cut off or played with.

Above: The claws, made from hardened skin rather than bone, are naturally sheathed when relaxed.
Top left and left: The detection of scent is critical to a cat's social interactions, while his eyesight is excellent in low light, helping to make him the perfect predator.

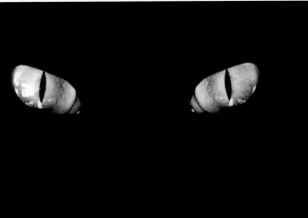

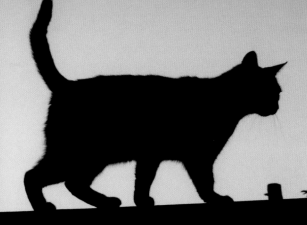

Above: Clusters of whiskers around the head and legs provide information about the cat's immediate surroundings.
Left: The position of the tail signals how a cat is feeling in a particular situation. It also helps maintain balance.

Communication

A cat's vocal range varies from warming purrs to ear-splitting caterwauls.

Vocalization Cats have an amazing repertoire of vocal noises to indicate their desires. In fact, approximately 16 different recognizable sounds have been distinguished in our domestic cat. Each cat will develop his own repertoire, depending upon his experiences and personal inclination. Most of these sounds are used to communicate intentions in close proximity to another individual. However, we are all aware of their ability to express themselves over longer distances by the use of caterwauling and yowls when mating or territory is at issue!

We don't yet fully understand how purring actually originates. It is thought that it's caused by the passage of air over the false vocal chords, which causes them to vibrate. A cat is able to change the intensity of his purr, depending on a situation and his response to it. Purring develops at a very early age and allows the kitten to signal to mom that all is well. Because the kitten can purr continuously while feeding, this is a perfect method of communication. The mother will also purr when she returns to her litter to signal her presence and to relax them. A kitten will make more types of noises as he matures. Deaf kittens, surprisingly, can still express the full range of kitten noises despite not having heard them for themselves.

Interpreting Your Cat's Body Language

Posture and Emotions Observing your cat's body posture will provide you with insight into how he is feeling and make you better able to respond appropriately. Normally a number of signs must be seen together to confirm an emotion. However, there are signals that you can look out for in the ears, whiskers and tail.

Ears Ear positions can express a lot about how your cat is feeling—ears are amazingly mobile. The following movements provide a rough guide to your cat's emotions, but you are likely to see a combination of behaviors which will tell you more precisely what the actual mood is.

Upright and tilted	Indicates relaxation
Facing and tilted backwards	Cat is anxious
Flattened backwards	Cat is fearful
Flattened to the side	Cat is fearful but aggressive
Straight up but twisted to the sides	Cat is angry and may be aggressive

*ght: This cat's eye focus
d ear and whisker
entations indicate where
s interest lies. The tail
rled around the body
dicates a fairly relaxed
ate of mind.*

Whiskers are an
important feature,
and your cat will
move them
according to his
activity and his
feelings
about a
situation.

*elow: The raised rump,
uffed tail, and ear
osition signal the tension
t by this cat in the
esence of another.*

Whiskers directly out from face in natural position	Contented, happy cat
Whiskers flat back against face	May be threatened or feeling aggressive
Whiskers held forward	If towards an item of interest, whiskers helping provide information

Tail The tail is also used to express emotions and can be "read"
by you, the owner.

*elow: The arched back,
ised fur, wide mouth,
nd lowered tail signal this
at's defensive-aggressive
sponse to an encounter.*

Full length, erect tail, held stiffly as he approaches	A friendly greeting gesture for well-known humans or companion cats.
Flicks of the tail tip	Indication of irritation
Wagging vigorously	Indecision or a prelude to a fight
Lowered tail with raised rump	Normally seen during an aggressive encounter with another cat
Puffed up tail carried low	Cat is fearful
Puffed up, arched tail accompanied by arched back	Displaying arousal and indecision between aggression and defence or escape—he may attack
Relaxed tail curled around body	Happy, contented cat
Tail tucked tightly around body	Defensive, nervy cat
Tail fully tucked under body	Complete submissive gesture often to signal defeat after a fight

LIFE STAGES

Queens and kittens

A pregnant female domestic cat (the queen) will spend time searching out a safe area to give birth to her litter. She won't actually make a nest but tries to find a quiet, dry place where the kittens are not at risk of being preyed upon. Pregnancy lasts approximately 63 days. Other related females in the group may help out with the care of the kittens.

When breeding cats, it's important to choose good-tempered parents, because their characters are likely to affect the kittens' temperaments. A kitten's tolerance of humans is inherited from his father, though the mother obviously has a strong influence on early learning. In addition, socialization will work with inherited traits to produce the final character. The queen is normally able to provide for her kittens, but a breeder does need to be aware of their development and ensure that all seem to be sucking properly, responding normally, and are in good physical condition.

Kitten development

Kittens are blind at birth and completely reliant upon their mother and other females in the group for care. Their eyes open at any time between two days and two and a half weeks after birth.

At approximately three weeks old, the kittens are ready to begin learning life-skills from their mother in earnest. Kittens learn by watching the queen, because they cannot move far from the nest until about four weeks of age. The first techniques learned, not surprisingly, involve predatory behaviors. Over the following weeks the kittens continue to observe their mother and by five weeks are displaying their own instinctive predatory reactions.

Above: *A mother cat, or queen, positions herself to make it easy for her kittens to feed.*

Far right: *The queen will take care of her kittens and ensure that they don't wander too far. She will respond to a distress call by collecting the kitten and returning it to the nest.*

Social play and interactions can be observed from four weeks of age, and the kittens continue to develop these skills until roughly 12 weeks. The more experiences he has during his early weeks, the more able a kitten will be to cope with future change and social relations. The breeder plays a critical role in ensuring that the kittens are exposed to as wide a range of encounters and environmental experiences as possible as well as making sure that they are all growing and developing normally.

Adolescence occurs very early in the domestic cat, and many owners are caught by surprise. A female cat may reach puberty at only four months, allowing variation for body condition and breed differences. Males can successfully mate between five and ten months of age.

SOCIALIZATION

In order for a cat to be well adjusted and happy to interact with his family, he needs to have plenty of positive experiences as a young kitten. We commonly call these experiences "socialization." Responses to new experiences as an adult also depend upon the amount and range of environmental experiences a cat has during his first seven weeks. We call this habituation or familiarization.

We now understand that the **prime time for socialization** in kittens actually occurs very early, between **two and seven weeks** of age. We call this the **"sensitive period"** of development. Poor socialization results in fearful responses later in life. Careful exposure to humans and other events during this time is essential. It's vital that the kittens do not experience extremely traumatic events during this time. Care should be taken when handling them and when introducing them to other household pets. Early medical treatment can also be problematic, and, in such a case, lots of careful handling and playing will be necessary to counteract any negative associations that might have been created.

Above: Having lots of pleasant encounters with people at a young age will help to prepare a kitten for life as a sociable adult.

The amount of gentle handling a young kitten experiences influences his level of social confidence later in life and the number of people with whom he will be sociable as an adult. Kittens that have been born and raised in a barn or shed are likely to be fearful of people because they will have had very little human contact. Kittens raised in a busy household or good cattery will have regular human contact and are more likely to present good social skills.

When your kitten first comes home, he might be a little shy until he finds his feet and gains some confidence. However, if your kitten has not been introduced to people during his first few weeks, then it's highly likely that he will retain his nervous character. A young kitten bonds with his new owners as if they were his parents. He will also build associations between his owner and the provision of valuable resources (such as food and shelter), thereby developing a strong attachment.

Far right: This kitten's arched back and puffed tail show his wariness toward his new housemate. If the dog is calm and controlled by his owner, then regular careful meetings will build the kitten's confidence and should allow peaceful and relaxed cohabitation.

Socialization should continue until the cat is fully mature; the first year is a good guide to a cat's mature character, though always remember that if your cat goes many years without experiencing people/handling/children, he will not necessarily feel relaxed when he encounters them again.

TRAINING YOUR CAT

Below: Rewarding desirable behaviors, such as calmly approaching this child, means this kitten is more likely to want to interact with her again.

It's still commonly thought that cats cannot be trained. However, although they do not perform like dogs, they are able to learn and make good or bad associations with events and actions, which means that their behavior **can** be shaped and altered. Most owners do some simple training without knowing it when they encourage their cat to come when called and then offer food or petting when he arrives.

Training cats is most successful when using **reward-based methods**.

Rewards

To reward your cat you will need to choose something that **your** cat loves. Most commonly this involves tasty food rewards, petting, or fun games with favorite toys. As the person who knows him best, you are probably in the best position to understand his desires. If you are unsure, then try lots of different things, but always be prepared to vary the reward as your cat's mood changes. Cats relish variety, both in terms of the task being taught **and** the reward on offer, so bear this in mind.

The timing of your reward must be accurate if you are to make good progress with your cat. This means that you must have the reward close at hand when he does the desired action. If he is made to wait too long for the reward (more than a few seconds), he will be confused and his interest will wane. Petting and praise are also useful rewards. However, make sure that your cat likes being stroked, or you may put him off.

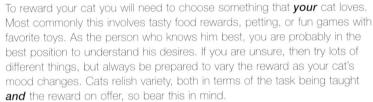

Any praise, petting, or rewards that your cat receives should encourage him to repeat whatever behavior he has just performed. Be careful not to offer these when he is doing something you dislike; so, for example, avoid stroking or feeding when your cat is meowing at you (unless you, your family, **and** the neighbors like the noise!)

Punishment

Punishment means the application of something aversive (that your cat dislikes) or the removal or something he likes. You must be very careful when trying to punish a cat. Some owners find themselves shouting at their pet when they discover he has done something wrong. A short shout, though hardly ideal, can effectively disrupt a behavior as it occurs, but shouting **after** the behavior has occurred and ended is totally ineffective. Interrupting an action with a shout may be instinctive, but make sure that your tone changes to a soothing one once your cat stops the unwanted behavior.

*Far right: Perfect timing is essential when using an interrupter to stop an unwanted activity. The aim is to momentarily startle your cat, **not** to terrify him.*

It is **never** appropriate to smack a cat. This will make him stressed and afraid. Any punishment or aversive event should not be associated with you. He must believe that his action has caused the unpleasant event to occur spontaneously.

The most effective "punishment" for a cat is a sudden interruption. This is something that suddenly occurs when a cat does a particular action, which startles or disrupts his activity. He should **not** link the event with **you**, because it's important that he feels comfortable and trusting towards you. Examples of this are: a sudden noise, something tossed **near** him (always choose a non-dangerous item such as a bean bag and **never** throw it **at** your cat), a quick squirt of water, or a hiss of compressed air. You must take care that you don't threaten your cat with a water pistol or other item, or he may simply begin to perform the unwanted behavior when you are not around to use it, and his trust in you may be lost.

Reward your cat as soon as he performs a desirable behavior.

Interrupters should be immediately applied and easily linked to his activity.

Never punish **after** a naughty action has ended. If you missed it, then you are too late to take action.

elow: Select food
*wards that your cat can't
sist, but avoid large treats,
he'll probably grow bored
feel full too soon.

Above: Soft bean bags **may
sometimes** be useful to disrupt
some unwanted behaviors
but should only be considered
if you have consistently tried
other training and management
methods first.

Equipment Various products can act as effective interrupters for naughty behavior. Compressed air canisters (such as those for cleaning cameras or computer keyboards) can emit a hiss that cats respond to quickly. Of course, they should never be aimed at your cat—the noise itself should disrupt the behavior effectively. Other remote products are available that emit a sound or spray when you either press the remote control or when the cat himself triggers the sensor. The benefit of these products is that you can be out of sight and so cannot be linked with the unpleasant event. Please note: these can be useful in certain situations, but it's always best to discuss these options with your behaviorist so that any anxiety problems are not worsened. You must also address the reason for the behavior manifesting itself in the first place, or your cat may simply relocate or become more stressed.

Withdrawal of Pleasurable Event Another option is to withdraw something your cat likes when he does something you dislike. The best method with cats is to withdraw petting and attention when your cat does something undesirable. Be careful not to stroke or soothe him while he is performing an unwanted action.

Above: Some unwanted behaviors can be disrupted by the hiss from a compressed air canister. This should not be used to address fear- or anxiety-based problems. The canister should be held discreetly and never used to threaten or scare.

Time Out This means that you remove the cat from your presence. It is useful when a cat continues to demand attention, repeats the unwanted action, or is too wound up to interact with. This allows him to calm down while you relax and rethink how to address the problem. Some cats can be lifted and put out of the room, whereas others may need to be guided out with a blanket or cushion if the level of arousal means they are likely to scratch or bite. In some situations it may be best if you leave the room.

Below: Your cat will probably like the reward of petting and cuddling, though you should be careful when trying to stroke him after he's been aroused or overexcited.

REWARDS	PUNISHMENT
• Always reward a good behaviour immediately	• Never smack your cat
• Find a reward that your cat likes.	• A short, sharp shout should be all that's needed
• Be prepared to vary the reward	• Stop petting or stroking if your cat is doing something naughty at the same time
• Ensure the reward can be accessed quickly	• Use an interrupter to disrupt your cat from a naughty behavior, then praise him for stopping
• Set your cat up to succeed as often as possible	• Don't hold grudges—your cat is not out to "get you" or to deliberately annoy you

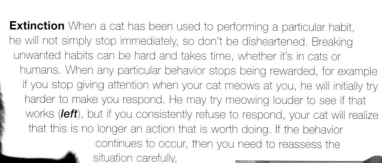

Extinction When a cat has been used to performing a particular habit, he will not simply stop immediately, so don't be disheartened. Breaking unwanted habits can be hard and takes time, whether it's in cats or humans. When any particular behavior stops being rewarded, for example if you stop giving attention when your cat meows at you, he will initially try harder to make you respond. He may try meowing louder to see if that works (*left*), but if you consistently refuse to respond, your cat will realize that this is no longer an action that is worth doing. If the behavior continues to occur, then you need to reassess the situation carefully, because it's likely that your cat is still getting some kind of reward or response that he likes. Make sure everyone in the household is following the same rules.

Training

Far right: Making use of your cat's natural instincts is the best way to succeed in training as he'll be keen to be involved.

Cats can be taught simple tricks by a patient owner using desirable rewards. Your cat must be relaxed with you and happy in the area where you want to train. You can lure him with food or a cat wand (a long thin wand to which an attractive lure like a feather or ribbon is attached, normally by string) and teach him to touch, stretch, and jump. Cats don't like to have to repeat the same behavior too many times, so vary your lesson and keep it short. Cats will not remain interested as long as dogs, and they certainly cannot ingest the same quantity of food rewards, so short interesting sessions should maximize your chance of success.

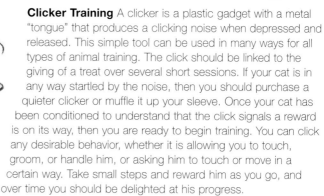

Clicker Training A clicker is a plastic gadget with a metal "tongue" that produces a clicking noise when depressed and released. This simple tool can be used in many ways for all types of animal training. The click should be linked to the giving of a treat over several short sessions. If your cat is in any way startled by the noise, then you should purchase a quieter clicker or muffle it up your sleeve. Once your cat has been conditioned to understand that the click signals a reward is on its way, then you are ready to begin training. You can click any desirable behavior, whether it is allowing you to touch, groom, or handle him, or asking him to touch or move in a certain way. Take small steps and reward him as you go, and over time you should be delighted at his progress.

PREVENTING INAPPROPRIATE BEHAVIOR

Lower left: Facial pheromones are commonly rubbed from the cheek area onto items in places where the cat feels particularly comfortable and relaxed.

Cats like routine and so will adapt to your daily pattern, provided that their basic feline needs are being met. Once they have developed a habit, it can be hard for them to change, so it's advisable to deal with any unwant behaviors as soon as they occur.

When a cat experiences something pleasurable, it's likely that he will to repeat whatever the activity was in order to get more reward. Therefore you see your cat doing something you like, then ensure that he knows it's good activity. Praise and petting will help encourage him to repeat that behavior again.

Pheromone Therapy

Advances in science have provided us with many means to improve our pet's environment. We know how important smell is to cats and namely ho important their familiar pheromones (natural chemical substances secreted by animals that are used to communicate between members of the same species) are to a feeling of relaxation and familiarity. There are commercial available products based on **feline facial pheromones** that can be introduced into your home via plug-in diffusers and/or sprayed onto speci items, depending upon the problem. These products are available from yo veterinarian and from pet sites online. If you are unsure of which one to us or what your cat's problem actually is, then consult a qualified behaviorist, who will be able to help.

Above: Choose the reward that your cat likes best. Some adore petting, others don't.

Seeking additional help This is often necessary for behavior problems. Ask your veterinarian to refer you to a qualified behaviorist who has experience in dealing with feline problems. It's important to seek profession advice rather than haphazardly try various suggestions from friends and

neighbors or ideas seen on the television, because it's essential that **your** cat's problem be diagnosed correctly. Two cats may perform similar behaviors for completely different reasons, and what works to solve one problem can be unhelpful or cause distress in another. Since your cat is an individual and your household is unique, so too should be your behavioral modification program when the problem is extreme or well-developed. This book will provide ideas and suggestions for a range of problems, but please do seek help where it's indicated that you should or when your cat's problem has existed for a long period of time and/or it's causing him or your family distress.

Above: *It's important to remember that any behavior that you encourage is likely to re-occur. If you respond to meowing by your young cat, it's likely that he'll use meows to request food or attention in the future.*

HELPFUL HINTS—DO'S AND DON'T'S

- Don't physically punish your cat by smacking or hitting him with an object or by scruffing or shaking him. Your cat will associate you with this negative experience and will start to avoid you and perhaps begin displaying more undesirable behaviors, such as aggression, inappropriate toileting, or spraying, or he may simply become impossible to handle because of fear.

- Do make sure your cat has plenty of opportunity to express his feline instincts. Enrich his environment with toys, hiding places, and feeding stations, and ensure he has adequate social interaction to provide stimulation (with you if there are no other cats in the house).

- Do be consistent in the way you interact and the rules you instil, because this is the only fair way to own a cat.

Above: *Enriching your cat's environment can involve simple items such as paper bags, which provide hiding places and opportunites for games.*
Left: *If you are concerned by any of your cat's behavior, then arrange a veterinary examination to rule out medical problems and to obtain a referral to a feline behavior specialist.*

What if my cat is being weaned?

1 Kittens can begin to ingest solid food at four weeks, and at this time they begin to be weaned from their mother. This is a natural and necessary process. The breeder will begin to offer some solid kitten food, and this will replace the kitten's need for the mother's milk. In a natural situation the mother will bring solid foods back to the litter for them to eat. Kittens are typically weaned completely by seven weeks of age, though some mothers, particularly those with single kittens, will continue to feed for longer. You don't need to feed your kitten cow's milk when you bring him home; in fact, many cats are intolerant to lactose and suffer from gastric complaints when fed dairy milk.

What if my cat was hand-reared?

2 It's true that mother knows best. When kittens have been removed from their mother very early, their development can be hindered. They can be more excitable and sensitive to stimuli. Owners often find that these kittens play very roughly and bite much harder than kittens reared to weaning age by the queen. This seems to be because they haven't had the appropriate feedback during play development and because they have often learned that people (and their hands or feet in particular) are items onto which they can direct their play. This can be very difficult to cope with, especially around children or elderly people. In such cases kittens need to be encouraged to play appropriately with toys starting as early as possible. Games should stop as soon as the kitten tries to swipe or bite at hands. Other kittens are overly attached to the person that reared them. These kittens also need to be encouraged to play independently and spend time away from that person, or it may be very difficult for them in the future when that person is not around.

What if my cat is very young but plays roughly with his siblings or charges around the home?

3 It is normal for kittens between the ages of three and four months to be involved in extremely interactive play, such as chasing, running, and play-fighting. This can be alarming, especially if you are not used to cats or if your kitten has replaced a very elderly cat who led a quiet and restrained life.

These behaviors should not be punished, but neither should they be rewarded. Things normally calm down again if your kitten gets enough stimulation elsewhere. Provide him with plenty of toys and at least one cat station upon which he can climb and enjoy some fun exercise. He should have access to suitable toys throughout the area where he is allowed to roam, because he will need to play frequently and will otherwise focus on items that may be fragile or valuable.

hat if my cat a pedigree?

4 There are over 70 registered breeds of cat. A pedigree means that the cat has ancestry that can be traced back over many generations, and all those individuals were of known pedigree type. Picking a pedigree will allow you to research the type of cat that you most prefer and that will fit into your home and lifestyle best. Although all cats are individuals, there are many traits among cats of the same pedigree that may influence your choice. Some breeds are active and more tenacious than others. Some have greater predispositions to certain health or behavior problems. For example, Persian cats are more likely to present house-soiling problems than other breeds. Siamese and oriental breeds are naturally more vocal. No breed need be a problem if the cat's needs are being met. Different breeds will have different needs. Consider all the traits and try not to be influenced by looks alone.

Pedigree kittens often remain with their breeder well beyond the seven-week period, so you must ensure that the breeder has tried to provide a thorough early socialization and habituation as described earlier in this chapter. The kittens should have had regular handling by a variety of people before coming home to you so that they feel comfortable around their new family.

If you socialize your pedigree cat well so he is comfortable around people and new places, you may be interested in taking him along to cat shows. Your breeder will be able to advise you on the suitability of your cat and will explain the entry process.

bove: A thorough cialization makes it sier for a cat to cope h a busy lifestyle.

What if my cat is very young but is naughty already?

5 Remember that your kitten has a natural urge to perform and practice feline behaviors. Some of these are less suitable for life within a human family, but it's essential that you make time to help teach your young cat what is expected from him. Never simply assume that he knows rights or wrongs or that he is making mistakes out of spite. If you don't teach your cat what you like, then you can't feel cross if he gets it wrong. You can only expect so much from a kitten, so be realistic and take the time to train him to behave nicely.

r right: Rough and nble play between ens allows them to actice and perfect the aneuvers they may need er in life in both hunting d in certain social uations.

What if my cat is not a pedigree?

6 The majority of cats fall into the regular house cat category. When two different pedigrees are bred together, the kittens are called crossbreeds. Cats that come from no clear breed type are described according to their physical looks, e.g. domestic shorthair or domestic longhair. The lack of a pedigree bears no relation to the amount of pleasure you will gain from your cat. Factors that are import to pedigree and regular domestic cats alike are parental temperament, a thorough socialization and good health.

What if my cat is a rescue cat?

Above: *A rescue cat can make a wonderful pet.*

7 There are many fabulous cats who, through no fault of their own, have ended up in rescues. Some of these will have pedigree backgrounds and some will have had perfect socializations. Othe may have had little contact with humans or other cats. Ask the rescue to give you as much information as possible about the type of life the cat has had previously, how he interacts with the staff in the shelter, and, if possib visit him several times to get to know him. Remember that cats in shelters are often feeling anxious from being enclosed and in a new environment th they have not experienced before. Take your time and consider all the cats the cattery; remember that some will feel stressed and will therefore not se themselves as well as others, but this does not necessarily mean they will not make great pets.

Some shelters will have a quiet room or enclosure where you can mee the cat you like and get to know him a little before making up your mind. If the cat you are considering homing did not have a perfect early start, he is not necessarily going to be unsuitable. He is less likely to be confident in a wide range of social situations, but this may not mean that he won't mak a great pet. A timid cat can learn to interact with and adore his owners an can live very happily in certain home environments. This book will provide advice about ensuring your cat can become as relaxed as possible.

What if my cat is feral?

8 A feral cat is not simply one that is living free, nor is it a genuine wild cat. It is a domestic-type cat that has been born and bred ir the wild and has not had any socialization and handling by huma Feral cats are normally extremely fearful of people, though occasionally so will develop a trust in a particular handler over time. If you have homed a feral kitten, you or the rescue must spend his early weeks (ideally before five weeks) carefully handling and teaching him to relax around you by usir food, games, and gentle handling. Without this, the kitten is likely to grow frightened of people and may be extremely aggressive when approached. Mature feral cats are normally happiest to be left to live the life they know and understand, though it's wise to follow a TNR (Trap-Neuter-Release) program so he does not add to the ever-growing feral and stray population through breeding.

What if my cat doesn't purr?

9 Some cats are more vocal than others. Some purring is simply too quiet for the human ear. If your cat is angry or irritated, then purring is less likely.

What if my cat purrs all the time?

Right: Nothing quite signals contentment like a purring cat, though owners should be aware that purring can continue despite pain or injury.

10 A purring cat is a delightful sound to hear. Purring begins when the kitten is a mere two or three days old, although it's hard to hear at this stage. Cats can purr continuously while breathing in or out. Purring acts to signal contentment, but it's important to know that it can occur even when a cat is in pain, ill, or distressed. Purring has also been noted as a sign of friendship, as a signal of a relationship, or as an indication of friendly intent if the cat is feeling unsure of itself.

What if my cat chatters his teeth?

11 Teeth chattering often occurs just prior to a cat's pouncing on his prey (it can be a toy). It's probably a result of pent-up excitement and tension prior to the predatory response as well as being part of the action cats make when biting their prey. Despite not actually performing a real kill, some cats seem unable to inhibit this response. Your cat might chatter if he becomes very aroused while watching birds or squirrels in the yard, or even on TV!

35

What if my cat blinks at me?

12 Cats use slow eye blinks as a calming signal to others and to signal peaceful contentment. Sometimes they seem to simply hood their eyes in our presence. Since staring at your cat is perceived by him as a rather alarming and threatening gesture, it's a good idea to engage in some natural feline signals yourself if your cat seems a little nervous. Avoid direct eye contact, slowly blink, and hopefully you should see your cat relax.

What if my cat wags his tail at me?

13 Tail movements can signal many moods. A relaxed tail generally signals a relaxed cat, but a twitching or wagging tail signals that your cat is becoming aroused and may become reactive. Think about what you are doing when he is wagging his tail, because he may be feeling unsure and a little stressed. If you are petting him and his tail begins to wag, then it's advisable to remove your hand quietly and slowly and allow him to calm again.

Right: Cats have an unusual tail tip that can move independently of the main length. A flicking tail signals that the cat may soon react.

What if my cat meows a lot?

14 Interestingly, cats tend to keep most meowing for communicating with their owners. Very few meows occur between cats. The tendency to be vocal will vary between individuals, although some breeds are much more talkative than others. Siamese are particularly vocal, and you must consider this when choosing one; so, too, are many of the Oriental breeds. If you dislike meowing, then these breeds may not be suitable for you, because it's unfair to get annoyed or angry as a reaction to their natural behavior. Of course, even Oriental cats may learn to be more vocal than normal, which can become problematic even to an enthusiast!

Most cats learn that meowing is a reliable way to gain response from their owner. When they are kittens their mewing makes us respond quickly to make sure they are happy. Cats are clever enough to realize that meowing normally makes owners focus on them, feed them, or pet them. If your cat meows during the night, refer to "What if?" no. 67 for advice. Elderly cats may meow more frequently than when they were young (see "What if?" no. 160).

What if my cat curls his lip and bares his teeth?

15 This behavior is called flehmen and allows the cat to detect scents better by exposing them to his Jacobson's organ, an olfactory organ that can be found at the front of the roof of the mouth. The cat is then able to "taste" the smell. Scent is highly important to cats in all walks of life, so it's vital for them to be able to process scents in this advanced manner. Flehmen is less apparent in our domestic cat than in wild cats, which have greater need to detect the scents of other animals, but if you watch, you will see your cat do this when he comes across an object where another cat has left its scent. The Jacobson's organ is also linked to appetite and sexual behavior (it helps in the detection of females in season).

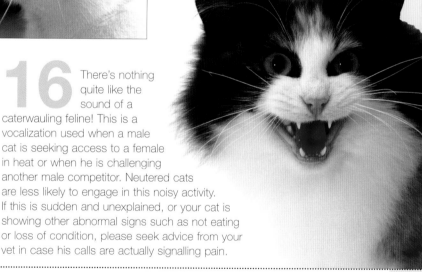

What if my cat caterwauls?

Above: By opening his mouth, the cat allows scents to flow over his Jacobson's organ, ready to be analyzed.

Right: A caterwauling choir of tomcats may group around a place where a female is in heat.

16 There's nothing quite like the sound of a caterwauling feline! This is a vocalization used when a male cat is seeking access to a female in heat or when he is challenging another male competitor. Neutered cats are less likely to engage in this noisy activity. If this is sudden and unexplained, or your cat is showing other abnormal signs such as not eating or loss of condition, please seek advice from your vet in case his calls are actually signalling pain.

What if my cat doesn't learn when I tell him off?

17 Scolding a cat is unlikely to result in the changes you desire. Cats don't belong to the type of social group in which members respond to this type of domineering relationship. The normal result is reduced confidence around you, avoidance behavior (which is a natural action that cats adopt to allow them to live in the same area without clashes occurring), and perhaps the triggering of spraying or marking. It's better to create distractions when you spot your cat doing something you dislike and teach him to do something else. If your cat loves your focus more than treats or a toy, you can punish unwanted attention-seeking behavior by walking away and leaving him alone for a short time.

HABITS AND MISHAPS AROUND THE HOME

PART

2

CONTENTS

What if my cat . . .

INTRODUCTION

Although cats are extremely popular pets, their activities around the home can sometimes cause concern. Use the questions and answers set out in this section to find out why your cat performs certain actions, and learn how to change his behavior before your relationship breaks down irreversibly.

INDOOR PROBLEMS

What if my cat scratches my furniture?

18

Scratching is part of natural feline behavior, and we cannot simply erase this instinct, however unfortunate the owners of some cats may find it. The purpose of scratching items is multifaceted: it allows visible territory marking, it spreads scent messages to other cats, and it helps to keep claws healthy by removing the outer sheaths. Stretching up to scratch also physically exercises muscles and tendons in the feet, which helps to keep the cat agile. Cats normally scratch around areas that are important to them within their "core territory," such as the places where they sleep, eat, and play in the home. As this is also part of the living area in our homes, this often means that furniture or fittings may be targeted. Some cats scratch around entrance areas (doors/kitty doors) or next to windows on the walls or curtains. This is typically territory marking, although cats who want to get outside to exercise may also do this out of sheer frustration.

Indoor cats are most likely to present with scratching problems because they have less opportunity to express themselves than outdoor cats, who typically scratch-mark fence posts and trees in the yard on a daily basis. Keeping cats indoors does not mean that their basic instincts disappear, so you must take this into consideration if you plan to keep your cat primarily indoors New cats in the territory or home can instigate an increase in marking behavior, as can sheer boredom, so you will need to assess your situation carefully in order to diagnose the reasons properly and redirect your cat's attentions satisfactorily.

Action: If your cat is scratching furniture or walls, you will need to provide him with plenty of other options to divert his attention. *Your cat may prefer either a vertical post or horizontal scratching pad; look at where he has been scratching on your furniture to help you decide which would suit him better.* Position your new scratching post in front of the damaged item, because this is obviously an area where he expresses the urge to scratch. Prevent further damage from occurring by blocking access to the damaged item or by covering it with foil, plastic sheeting, plastic carpet runners, double-sided sticky tape, or some other non-attractive material (having first made sure that this won't damage your furniture or hurt your cat). With his existing scratching area "out of bounds," he should then redirect his attention onto the nearby specially made post.

Feline play stations and sisal posts provide entertainment and suitable scratching areas and can be either purchased or, for the more adventurous owner, built at home. Make sure the scratching post is stable and strong enough to withstand energetic climbing and jumping. A vertical post should ideally be taller than your cat when he stands up on his hind legs to scratch, because this will allow him to exercise the muscles of his body and satisfy his scratching urges. Larger posts with corners can be more appealing because he can scratch down two sides at once. A flat pad can be made from corrugated cardboard or sisal and needs to be long enough so that your cat can stand at one end and stretch out to scratch on the surface.

New scratching posts or pads are sometimes not overly appealing to cats when they are first introduced because of their design or scent. Use a cat wand or string to excite him and lure him to swipe or pounce on the post. Spray or rub catnip on the post to encourage him to show an interest. **Never** try to make him scratch the post by pulling or forcing his paws onto it. ▶

Above left: *Even tiny kittens will begin to scratch, so it's important that they have appropriate posts provided.*

Below and left: *Soft furnishings provide perfect marking posts for cats. The visible damage and the scent marks left behind from foot glands attract the cat to return.*

Above and below:
Scratching items around the cat's home territory is necessary to help remove the outer sheaths from its claws, whereas the stretching action helps to keep muscles toned and healthy.

Remember: What looks nice to a human is probably not what attracts a cat, so allow the post to become frayed and well-used, because this will be far more enticing to him. If he isn't keen on the new tight material on a post, you can loosely drape some other more attractive fabric over it and allow him to scratch and tear it up. His attempts will introduce scent to the main post as well as loosening some threads from it, which will make it more enticing when the covering fabric is eventually removed. Once your cat is happy to claw the post instead of your furnishings, you can start to move it away from the furniture a few inches a day until it's in a suitable position.

For homes with multiple cats, it's advisable to position several cat stations/posts around the house so that each cat can express himself freely. Keep your cat's nails trimmed so that they are not needle-sharp, because this may also reduce any damage to your furniture.

If you catch your cat scratching, you can interrupt the behavior as it starts (see Part 1 for advice on the best way to interrupt bad behaviors). Then move him gently to the new post and encourage him to scratch there. Never smack or physically chastise your cat, or he will grow to distrust you. Remote disruptors can be useful *if* your cat has been provided with plenty of alternative scratching areas.

On a more general level, ensure that your cat has plenty of activities to keep him entertained so that he never feels frustrated or bored. Place a scratching post near his favorite sleeping area so that he can scratch as soon as he wakes up and wants to stretch.

Overall, it's much better to address the reasons **why** your cat may be scratching rather than focusing solely on the unwanted damage. This will help to reduce the chances that it will recur elsewhere.

Left: *Multi-cat homes should include several climbing and scratching stations so each cat has a chance to scratch without feeling inhibited by another's presence. Preferences vary between upright and horizontal posts, so it's important to provide a choice.*

What if my cat destroys my stair carpet?

19 This is a problem that blights many cat-owner relationships. Young cats zoom up and down stairs in a frenzy of claws and pulled threads, while owners cringe at the damage being inflicted on their carpets. This problem is more likely to crop up with young cats and more active breeds, especially those which don't have free access to the outdoors and, as a result, have lots of pent-up energy.

Action: Ensure that your cat has adequate scratching opportunities elsewhere, and provide a scratching post at the top and bottom of the stairs, too. Increase your cat's energy output by arranging active play sessions. Encourage your cat to chase and hunt small toys that you manipulate with strings. Use specially made interactive toys, such as the electronically controlled mouse that moves in a random, unpredictable way—these will entice your cat to leap and pounce in appropriate ways, even while you are away. If you spot your cat about to embark upon a "stair run," then disrupt the behavior with a clap or **leave** command, and then encourage him to do something else that's more acceptable.

What if my cat peels the wallpaper?

20 Shredding wallpaper is a terribly destructive and expensive behavior that can quickly result in a cat being banished to a rescue shelter. Scratching of the wallpaper may be due to marking behavior (see "What if?" no. 18), play behavior (perhaps a loose corner caught your cat's attention), or simply an attraction due to the constituents of the wallpaper paste. Some cats will discover a game with the wallpaper by accident and then also learn that it attracts attention from their owners.

Action: The first remedial option must always be to make sure that your cat is getting enough stimulation in other areas of his life. Distract him away from the torn wallpaper and provide other games. Place a scratching post in the

area most targeted. It can be a good idea to secure clear, hard plastic sheeting against the affected walls until your cat learns that his attempts to scratch walls no longer result in the satisfaction that they previously did. In homes where numerous cats live and scratch-mark, corner protectors can be affixed to papered walls to prevent damage.

Left: Simple games with household objects can be entertaining and stimulating, and this helps to direct an energetic cat's focus away from undesirable behaviors.

43

What if my cat toilets around the house?

21

Firstly, have your cat's health checked to rule out any current medical problems, because most instances of sudden onset of inappropriate indoor toileting are due to bladder or urinary infections or disorders such as FLUTD (Feline Lower Urinary Tract Disease). Veterinary tests may be needed to identify an infection. Recent urinary tract problems can result in your cat wanting to avoid his litter box or regular toileting area because of negative associations with the pain he felt during urination. Infections can also result in your cat feeling the need to urinate much more often than normal. This urgency may mean that he's caught short and has to toilet in the nearest available place. If your cat is completely healthy, then you need to ask a number of questions:

Firstly, **where** should your cat toilet? If this is in a litter box, then ensure it's positioned correctly. Understandably, your cat may not want to toilet in the busiest area of the house or next to a glass door or window where he may be viewed by other cats or people. Your cat might use his box when the area is quiet but might choose another place when everyone arrives home from work or school. Similarly he won't want to toilet where he feels threatened by other family pets (or hovered over by the dog with unmentionable feeding habits). If tensions exist between your household pets, you will need to address this and provide more boxes **in different areas**. Some cats will happily share a litter box, but if the cats are not close friends this causes stress. Is the box near eating or drinking areas? Cats dislike toileting and feeding in the same location, so a rearrangement will be necessary. If the litter box has been moved recently, then your cat needs to know where it has gone. Take him and show him, likewise if he's a new cat. If he is elderly and forgetful, then you will need to move the box to somewhere that is very easily accessible.

Can your cat **access** his box? Your cat may need a clear pathway to the litter box. Elderly or unwell cats may find climbing into a high-sided tray difficult and may no longer be able to access tucked-away areas, such as in cupboards at the other end of the house. Likewise, older or arthritic cats may have trouble getting outside quickly enough to avoid accidents.

- Does your cat **feel comfortable** using his box? Your cat may dislike the type of litter you have chosen. What looks and smells good to humans may not be ideal for your cat. A highly scented, absorbent litter is often picked by owners who are then tempted to delay cleaning (see "What if" no. 22 for further explanation). He may have a preference for a certain type of box, whether it be deep, shallow, open, or with a lid. Remember that your cat's sense of "clean" may differ from your own. **His** is the opinion that counts. Many will, understandably, refuse to toilet in a soiled box. After all, people go to great lengths to avoid a dirty toilet, so we should understand why a cat may choose not to use the same soiled area repeatedly. It's not sufficient to simply scoop out soiled clumps and top up the litter day after day. You must replace soiled litter every day, if

Above: Cats like specific toileting places, but providing a suitable place takes careful thought and continued maintenance. You need to choose the right style of tray and type of litter, find a safe location, and then ensure regular cleaning. If you own several cats, then you may have to cater to their different preferences.

ove: There may be a dical reason for your 's inappropriate toileting, consider having a erinary check first.

low: Cats dislike ving to wait in line, so if litter box is already cupied, a cat might feel ced to go elsewhere.

not twice daily, and all boxes need to be completely emptied and cleaned thoroughly a couple of times a week, and more often if several cats are using it. Using tray liners can also be disconcerting to some cats as they can be upset by the plastic scent or by the sensation when they catch their claws while scraping the litter.

- In multi-cat households there should be sufficient boxes to suit all preferences. Some cats prefer a two-box system where you place both boxes together. This allows him a choice of which box to use until you get to clean them out. Even with two boxes daily cleaning is required.

- Your cat may have learned to avoid the box if you needed to medicate him and took the chance while he was positioned on his box. Many owners use this opportunity with less manageable cats, and inadvertently this causes a toileting problem.

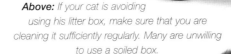

Above: *If your cat is avoiding using his litter box, make sure that you are cleaning it sufficiently regularly. Many are unwilling to use a soiled box.*

If your cat is meant to toilet outside, then you also need to answer some questions:

- Can your cat easily get **outdoors**? Sometimes the simple fact that your cat cannot get outside when he feels the need leads to his feeling forced to find an indoor toilet. Ensure the kitty door is open for long enough each

Below: Your cat needs to have easy access to his outside latrine area, such as this patch of soil.

day or that someone is home to let him out. Cats often toilet during the night during their active stage. If this is when he is locked safely inside, yo will need to provide a box. Older cats may need to be let out more often or at least have easy access to a box. Consider whether your cat feels confident using the kitty door. Are there other cats in the house, or are there neighborhood cats that may be preventing your cat from leaving? If so, you may need to provide more ways for your cat to get outside. Cat ramps from windows or careful positioning of plant pots to screen the fla can increase your cat's confidence as he emerges into the outside world. (See also "What ifs?" nos. 49 and 91.)

- Does your cat **feel safe outside**? If your cat normally toilet in the garden and has suddenly changed his pattern of behavior, then consider what is occurring in the area. Garde renovations, traffic disturbance, bullying by cats or frights from dogs, lawn sprinklers, and cat-scarers can all cause your cat become unwilling to leave the home. Such stress is linked t a condition known as **idiopathic cystitis**, which makes th cat need to urinate more often.

If your cat is toileting in the house because he's too nervous go outside, then it will be a good idea to provide a litter box while you address how to help the cat overcome the outdoor fears. However, make sure the box is not too close to a door th

Below: A covered litter box can provide a secure, private area, but owners need to pay particular attention to a regular cleaning regime so that scent levels don't build up.

may suddenly burst open or a kitty door that may be used by another cat.

- If your cat is new to the house, make sure that the box is easily accessible. He might not feel confident enough to explore your home immediately to find a litter box in the position you have chosen.

Dealing with severe problems: While your cat has free access to move around your home as he pleases, he is likely to continue soiling in the wrong areas. Cats are creatures of habit. Confining your cat in a single room with a litter box can help to retrain him to use the correct location and can be useful if the problem has been established for some time. If possible, this room should have flooring that is easy to clean and which contains no tempting alternatives to the box. In extreme cases it can help to place some of the material that your cat has been toileting upon inside the box. For example, a square of the soiled carpet alongside the litter you wish to change to. Gradually reduce the amount of material there while increasing the cat litter so he gets used to using the desirable product. Place a bed and a water bowl as far away from the litter box as possible. Gradually expand his area, under supervision, until he can be trusted again.

Kittens will naturally toilet in a litter box if they have easy access to it and it's clean. This desirable behavior is often taken for granted by owners, and we forget to encourage the cat to repeat the good behavior. Always reward behaviors you like, but wait until your cat has finished toileting before going over and petting him. Some cats may be upset by this interruption of their privacy, and it might discourage them from using the box while you are home. Calm praise is a good idea, but leave the main rewards for later.

Change the perceived purpose of the soiled areas by placing food bowls or water dishes on the spot instead. Once bad habits have been forgotten, you can gradually move the bowls to a more convenient location.

Punishment often results in a cat that becomes afraid to toilet in his owner's presence. In this scenario the cat simply continues to toilet during times when his owner is not around, which means the problem continues to grow. **Never rub your cat's nose in any mess** he has made. This old-fashioned technique will cause your cat more distress and may make him even more likely to toilet in the wrong area. Scolding your cat when you discover soiling is not advisable either, because he will begin to feel anxious around you. Either try to disrupt him when he begins to toilet in the wrong place, or temporarily confine him as described above so mistakes are avoided. ▶

Below: Kittens can be quickly toilet-trained if they have easy access to a litter box and if they're given opportunity to observe their mother using it. They will also practice covering feces, which leads to good habits in the future.

How to Clean a Litter Box

1 Clean the new box before placing it out for the first time to remove any scents remaining from its manufacture or from the pet store.

2 It's tempting to use the strongest cleaning products available, but some are not ideal. Avoid detergent-based products and heavily scented products. Remember that your cat has an acute sense of smell, and some products may be unbearable for him. Diluted bleach is an ideal product to use and is safe if rinsed off the litter box properly. (Please note that this is **not** useful for washing down soiled carpets or sprayed areas for reasons that will be explained below.)

3 Rinse several times with clean, warm water.

4 Allow the tray to dry in the air. (Pregnant or breast-feeding women should take extra precautions when cleaning cat litter boxes in order to avoid infection by toxoplasmosis, which is caused by a parasite that lives in the cat's intestines. It is dangerous to a developing human fetus. Though it's rarely caught from cats, it is as well to have an awareness of this as a potential risk. Good standards of hygiene and wearing rubber gloves are recommended.)

Cleaning a Soiled Area

1 Scrape up any feces or soak up excess urine with a cloth.

2 Scrub down with a dilute solution of powdered laundry detergent with enzyme (test an area first for color fastness) or a commercially available pet-accident cleaner. These enzymatic cleaners are good products but do take time to work to their full capacity, so you will need to block off the area from your pets. Covering up the area with a strongly scented cleaner will mask the scent from human noses, but it will still be obvious to your cat, who may want to return to the marked area and use it again, and ammonia-based products, such as bleach, can actually attract your cat back to the site. Enzymatic cleaners are able to break down the waste material and ensue that the waste products are completely eliminated.

3 Spray pet odor neutralizer over the soiled area, and then cover it with a plastic sheet or close off the room until it's dry to prevent your cat from being attracted by the damp floor.

Tip: Rubbing alcohol is excellent to wipe down soiled or sprayed surface after cleaning. As it evaporates, the remaining traces of urine are removed too. Wash down afterwards with clean water. Always follow the safety instructions on any product you use.

Note: Occasionally a cat will mark his territory by squatting and urinating on a horizontal surface. This ca be confusing and may be mixed up with a litter box problem. Often it can be determined by studying his other behaviors, toileting habits, and the locations of t soiling. Keep a written record of how an inappropriate toileting or marking problem progresses. This will provide

Below: It is sensible to wear rubber gloves when cleaning a cat's litter box. Cats' feces may harbor parasites than can be harmful to humans.

What if my cat is picky over types of litter in the box?

valuable information about the development of the problem and what the likely cause could be. Location is an important clue to discover what is triggering the problem.

22 A cat will often prefer the litter he'd been used to as a young kitten. Due to the array of types, packages, and offers available, owners will often change the product they buy, sometimes without even realizing. Long-haired cats often dislike clay or other clumping products because they stick to the hair on their feet, legs, and tail. A cat with a painful urinary infection may develop a negative association with the litter because he won't understand what is causing the discomfort. Some cats simply prefer the scent or texture of certain products, and some certainly do soak up urine better or can be scraped over feces easier than others. Where possible, stick to the same type of litter in order to cause as little disruption as possible to the cat's toileting routine.

If you do need to change the type of litter, do so over a period of about a week, and proceed by swapping a little of the current brand with some of the new product until the box only contains the new type. Always use a product that is tested as safe in case he accidentally ingests some litter. This is likely, because cats will lick their paws and coat, and kittens may ingest some while exploring their environment. Don't favor a highly scented product because it masks the urine scent from your senses. It's much better and less problematic to remove all soiled litter more frequently.

Far right: Modern litter products can help to eliminate unpleasant scents, though you must continue to scoop out any debris daily.

Below right and left: Clumping cat litter is made from an array of materials that should be non-toxic, easy to clean, and environmentally friendly.

49

What if my cat doesn't bury his feces?

23 The action of scraping and burying bodily waste is innate although arguably less important in domestic cats. Its original purpose was probably to help reduce detection by predators by covering the scents. It's likely that burying also improved disease and parasite control within core territory areas. Toileting habits can also vary between individuals. Confident cats leave more surface evidence, while more nervous individuals tend to bury.

The action of digging in litter substrate is probably initiated by the kitten observing the mother. If the kittens don't get this exposure, they may not necessarily perform this behavior as adults. This is especially true if the kitten has limited access to an appropriate litter to practice the behavior.

If the cat dislikes the litter you have provided, then covering of feces may not occur. Watch him to see how he behaves when using the box. He may avoid the litter, shake his paws, seem to fidget around, and take a long time to get positioned on the box. He may not fully enter the box, just edging his bottom over the side. Make sure that the litter is deep enough for him to scrape and bury his feces. Using more litter may seem like a waste, but this will help him fulfil this natural behavior and will also help absorb more of the odor.

What if my cat toilets in my indoor plant pots?

24 Cats can find the loose soil in our indoor plant pots extremely enticing and may begin to use them as latrine areas instead of/as well as going in their box or outdoors. Soil is absorbent, easy to dig, and pots are normally in convenient places where the cat feels safe. Simple solutions are to place large decorative pebbles, broken shells, or pinecones, on the soil, or even to fit wire mesh over the surface of the soil so your cat learns that this area is no longer comfortable to use as a toilet. At the same time, investigate the problem to make sure that there are no reasons why your cat is not wishing to toilet outdoors or in his own litter box.

What if my cat won't use his new covered litter box?

25 Covered litter boxes normally come equipped with a lid and often a flap through which the cat has to enter his enclosed toilet area. A new covered box can be hard for a cat to get used to if he has only ever experienced a simple open tray. Some cats prefer the security and privacy of a covered box, but often this style is chosen to fit in with our human preferences—we prefer to avoid seeing and smelling urine and feces. A covered box tends to be cleaned out less often than an open tray, which is not acceptable to your cat. Odors quickly build up inside the box, especially those with a cat-flap door.

If you are determined to use this type of box, then keep as many features as similar as possible by using the same litter as in the original box. Place the new box where the old tray was located. Gently show your cat how to enter the box and, if possible, leave the flap open at first. If your cat doesn't seem to understand that the box is a toilet, then place a little urine soiled litter on top of the new fresh litter to stimulate toileting instincts. If your cat continues to avoid using the covered box, you may have to go back to the original one, which will quickly rectify any problems and allow the old routine to be re-established.

What if my cat misses the litter box?

26 Some owners find that their cat will happily go to the box to toilet but will then "miss." If this is a sudden change of behavior, then *please seek veterinary help*, because if your cat is feeling pain while urinating or defecating, he might move around or fail to squat properly. A surprising number of cats actually have arthritis, which makes it harder for them to squat properly. Ensure that the box is large enough and can be easily entered. A covered box or a box placed inside a cardboard box set on its side can help keep the cat confined and prevent any feces or urine from landing inadvertently on the floor. Make sure that your cat likes the type of litter you have chosen, or he may avoid standing in the box (see "What if?" no. 22).

What if my cat can't easily be identified as the culprit with toileting or spraying problems?

27 Identifying which cat in a multi-cat household is responsible for a toileting or spraying problem can be extremely difficult. Isolating your cats from one another may be helpful, but if the marking behavior or litter box avoidance is a result of conflict between the cats, then splitting them up can actually resolve the problem temporarily, leaving you with the same confusion when you reintroduce them. Setting up a camcorder can help, but capturing evidence may be tricky if the problem cat is toileting in a variety of places, or camcorder battery life may pose limitations since it may take a long time before he does eliminate in the wrong place. If you are still in doubt about which cat is defecating away from the box, you may wish to give him a few drops of harmless green food dye with his meal so his stools will be distinguishable from the others.

Action: One solution your vet may be able to help you with is the provision of a fluorescent dye, which is given to one cat at a time. The cat's urine will fluoresce when viewed under an ultraviolet lamp. Where there are only two cats, it may be advisable to give the least likely culprit the treatment first, or you may be disturbed to find your whole home glowing when you turn on the ultraviolet lamp!

Left: The characteristic body posture of a spraying cat is very easy to identify; the tail will rise and quiver, and he'll turn his back against the targeted object.

What if my cat defecates around the home?

28 Uncovered feces deposited away from the normal toileting area can sometimes be left as signals to mark territory. This behavior is known as "middening" and can be recognized by the positioning of the deposits in areas near important locations. Cats that do this are often feeling stressed and are trying to signal their presence to other cats or even to people. This can be treated as other marking problems (see "What ifs?" nos. 29 and 30). Defecating around the home could also result from litter box aversion or a problem with its location. See "What ifs?" nos. 21 and 25 for more information.

What if my cat sprays urine up the curtains?

29 Scent is highly important to cats, and urine spraying is used to mark territory and to leave olfactory messages for other cats in the area. Unfortunately, when a cat is experiencing social problems or general anxieties, spraying can occur within the home, which, as the core territory, is normally free from spray. Male and female cats can both be involved in a spraying problem (and almost all cats will spray outside), although intact males are the most common culprits in problem spraying.

Marking behavior can be recognized and distinguished because the cat tends to sniff the area keenly, tread his feet, turn, hold his quivering tail upright, and then squirt a small amount of urine onto the chosen location. Urine spraying normally occurs up against vertical surfaces in this way and is often directed around windows and doorways or on landmarks perceived to be important by the cat. Spraying allows the cat's scent to be spread around the area and can help to make him feel more secure.

Spraying on your curtains often indicates that your cat is feeling threatened from something outside, perhaps when he sees neighborhood cats or even after the house has been invaded by a neighbor's cat. He may also spray on the window itself or on the walls to either side of it.

Action: Help to reduce his tension by blocking his view from the window so he does not see other cats outside, perhaps by spraying the lower portion of the window with temporary opaque window spray or by placing opaque plastic sheeting (such as can be used in bathroom windows) along the lower section to block his view while leaving a clear view above for humans. This method may seem less than aesthetically pleasing but is

Below: A cat will be interested in what's going on outside his home environment and may spend considerable time watching the world go by.

useful until the spraying problem is addressed. Dissuade him from using the window sill by preventing his access to it. You can also identify where other cats tend to sit outside and make changes to your yard in order to remove their viewing platform into your home. Growing small trees or shrub hedges may also help to add privacy in the longer term. Window planters can provide more cover for your cat and a better feeling of security.

Provide your cat with plenty of entertainment within the home. Clean any marked areas thoroughly with water and enzymatic cleaners or rubbing alcohol (test areas first to avoid discolouration or damage to surfaces). If your cat is a young uncastrated male, neutering has a very high chance of solving the problem. Females in season often present with a temporary spraying problem. If your cat is being bullied by another household cat, then consider their suitability as housemates. Offer more safe places where the bullied cat can hide, feed separately, and reduce any competition between the cats by providing different pathways for each cat to access and retreat from each resource so they don't have to meet face to face.

If the problem is stress-related, products obtainable from your vet such as the pheromone-based spray, which is a synthetic copy of a feline pheromone, can help reduce the likelihood of further spraying. This is sprayed onto the items once you have cleaned them properly. Remember to rinse thoroughly first, or your enzymatic cleaner may break down the pheromone product and reduce its efficiency.

If stress is causing your cat to perform any unwanted behaviors, changes to his environment will be necessary. If the stress is extreme, you may need to discuss anti-anxiety medication with your veterinarian or animal behaviorist, because this can help to boost the effectiveness of a behavioral program.

Above: Set aside time each day for play sessions to keep your cat entertained and happy.

Left: Cats can feel threatened when they see strange cats intruding into the space directly outside their home territory. This can lead to aggression, marking, or even extreme anxiety.

What if my cat sprays on my shopping bags or on the mail?

30

Spraying within the home indicates that the cat is feeling unsettled and anxious. Cats who feel particularly sensitive about territorial issues may be upset by the arrival of items that carry an array of unfamiliar scents into the home. The mail can bring odors from many locations directly into the home, as can scents brought in on the shopping. Both can both worry a sensitive cat. Plastic bags carry their own distinct smell, which seems to trigger some cats.

Strange cat odors may be picked up when you put your bags down on the pavement or on the step at your door to get your keys out; then you bring them straight into the home, and as a result your cat assumes another cat has invaded his territory. It's best to shut your cat away or distract him with an activity toy/food while you unpack and put away your shopping. Arrange for your mail to be placed in a mailbox attached to your house, or fix a mail net on the back of your door so letters are caught and held safely away from your cat.

Don't get angry, or he will probably feel more anxious and may spray elsewhere. If you see him about to spray, then stop him by creating a quick distraction such as by clapping your hands. When he startles and stops what he is doing, speak calmly to him and gently remove him from the scene.

Use a pheromone diffuser in the area to help calm down any tensions. Dealing with your cat's anxiety is obviously an important first step, but management of the problem can substantially reduce your stress, too.

Above: Scents carried on bags and clothing can be interesting to some cats but stressful for others.

Left: Neighborhood cat can leave their scents around the outside of your home, whether from marking, toileting, or simply stopping to rest. While many cats will take this apparent intrusion in stride, those with more sensitive temperaments may begin to spray item that bring such scents into their home.

What if my cat toilets in my briefcase or wash basket?

31

Although this problem can appear as though your cat has deliberately picked the most inconvenient place to eliminate in, it's very likely to have been caused by a litter box aversion. When the cat has no access to a box or cannot access it, he can be attracted by places that offer a space similar to a box. Bags and baskets offer privacy and the presence of papers or clothing allow the cat to cover any feces once he has finished. See "What if?" no. 21 for suggestions for ensuring that your cat feels comfortable using his box or going outdoors to toilet. Don't get angry or rub his nose in any mess. Until he resumes normal toileting habits, you should keep bags closed and shut away and cover any other tempting places. Remember that this alone will not stop the problem, because your cat can probably find many areas within the home to toilet. You have to deal with why he is not using the correct location first!

Right: If a litter box is unavailable, your cat may be attracted to another place which corresponds with his idea of a toilet.

What if my cat chews my paperwork?

32

When a cat chews or eats something that is inedible, such as paper, this behavior is called pica. Pica can occur when a cat is bored, hungry, playing, or stressed. Often the behavior occurs in front of the owners, suggesting that perhaps the cat has found something encouraging about their response. Attention-seeking is common, and you can reduce it by ensuring that your cat has plenty to do and is encouraged to play appropriately. Keep papers or other items out of reach while you change this habit. Make sure your cat is getting an adequate diet and is healthy, too. Be careful that he is not ingesting lots of ink-dye, which can be toxic. (See "What if?" no.148 for more veterinary advice about dealing with pica.)

Right: Nibbling on paperwork is a habit many cats will try out.

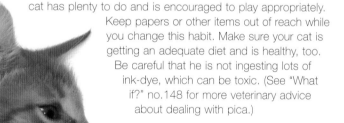

What if my cat chews my sweaters?

33

Some cats are particularly prone to sucking or chewing on material, especially wool. Breeds like the Siamese or related Oriental cats are often the culprits. This behavior can sometimes be linked back to problems when the kitten was weaned from his mother, but breeds like the Siamese seem to have a genetic predisposition towards this behavior. It's thought that the action of chewing or sucking is relaxing and pleasurable for the cat, and so the habit continues.

Wool-sucking is usually an annoying, though harmless, habit. However, for some cats it becomes extremely dangerous because they can actually ingest vast amounts of material that can cause intestinal blockages. Where genetic disposition or weaning problems are the culprits, if unmanaged this behavior will probably continue throughout the cat's life. These cats should not be bred. If the problem is extreme, it's worth combining a behavior modification plan with a course of drug therapy from your vet. The medication can help to regulate the reward-chemistry that this behavior stimulates and can allow you to break the cycle.

Action: The best way to limit the damage and prevent development of this problem is to keep woollen sweaters, scarves or blankets out of your cat's reach and to encourage him to participate in other activities where he can exercise and find more appropriate stimulation. Cats that have access to the outside are less likely to display wool-eating behaviors, so, if possible, create an outside enclosure for house cats. Redirect his desire to chew on material onto appropriate items, such as cat toys, safe gristly bones, or meat, and give him several small meals a day rather than one big one. Provide lots of alternative activities, such as playing with foraging toys, that will make him satisfied and contented. your cat seems to be developing a problem, it's worth seeking advice from an animal behaviorist.

Above: Take care if your cat chews on wool, because some will ingest dangerous amounts.

Far right: While some cats just play with wool, others develop an unhealthy chewing or sucking habit.

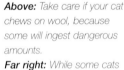

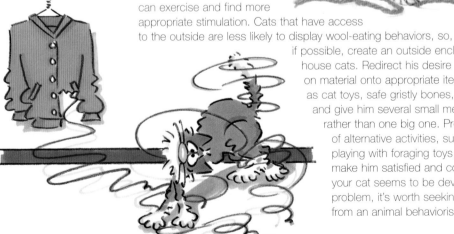

What if my cat eats my plants?

34

Cats do select some vegetation to supplement their diet. However, most houseplants and many garden varieties are not meant to be consumed and are easily damaged or may be poisonous to cats, even in small amounts. Some plants, like several of the lily varieties, can cause kidney failure and death within hours. Since these are becoming more popular in our gardens and in floral arrangements, it's recommended that owners should be highly aware of the dangers. **Even consuming tiny pieces of leaf or flower can cause death.** The pollen can get onto your cat's coat and be ingested during grooming, so they are never safe around your pet.

ght: Research the ety of your houseplants, cause some can be prisingly toxic. Ideally, place problem plants or ove them safely out of m's way.

elow: Common outdoor ants, such as daffodils, n also be problematic, pecially to young uisitive cats. Plant safe rieties to protect him m any potential danger.

Action: If your cat shows interest in eating plants, then place them in areas where he cannot get them to limit the risk. Try to buy only cat-friendly plants. Provide for your cat's requirements by planting your own cat grass in pots placed in areas he can reach so that he can find safe and tasty vegetation whenever he desires it. Cat grass seeds are available from gardening stores, supermarkets with plant sections, and online. (For veterinary advice refer to Part 5, "What if?" no. 139.)

What if my cat climbs the curtains?

35

Climbing the curtains is a tempting game for many young kittens who are practicing and developing their mobility skills. Older cats from more active breeds may also continue to do this. Indoor cats that do little to expend their energy tend to discover the excitement of this game.

However, apart from being an incredibly destructive pastime, this behavior can be dangerous. A cat may get his claws stuck or could get tangled in curtain pulls and strangle himself.

Action: You'll need to begin play times elsewhere when your cat has an opportunity to exercise; leaping and jumping after cat wands or a battery-powered toy would help to burn off excess energy. Restrict his access to the room while you are not there to supervize, and even consider tying your curtains up in plastic sheeting for a while until he has begun to focus on new games. Since he is obviously an avid climber, you should consider purchasing a specially made cat climbing frame or cat tree. These are tall, have several levels, and are designed to enrich your cat's environment. It's much better to provide for his needs than to focus solely on punishing him for being a cat.

Some people find success by hanging their curtains over the pole or lightly threading them up so that when the cat begins to climb, the curtains are pulled down. After a few attempts, the cat learns that this adventure is not worthwhile. At this point, the curtains can be hung properly again. Be very careful that the falling curtains don't spill curtain hooks, which your cat may swallow.

Remote movement sensors are available that can alert you every time your cat makes a move towards the curtains. Praise him for choosing not to play with the curtains, and keep encouraging appropriate games. Continue to vary his playthings and provide suitable activities even after the habit has stopped in order to reduce the likelihood of the problem recurring.

Below: Unfortunately, curtains make ideal climbing frames for active cats. Aside from the damage, dangers include getting tangled in pulls or trapped by a caught claw.

What if my cat has "mad" moments?

36 Many cats go through periods when they rush around the home as if being chased. They will wildly jump, grab with their claws, pounce, and run. Young cats are particularly prone to this behavior. Some cats who have restricted ability to express their natural feline behaviors will cope for certain lengths of time before simply *having* to release their frustrations. When they do so, the behaviors may seem out of place or inappropriate. If you have provided your cat with catnip-filled toys, then the rushing around that you are witnessing may be his natural feline response to the chemicals released by the plant (see "What if?" no. 56). Provide plenty of cat toys and close doors to rooms with lots of valuable ornaments or furniture. Most cats tend to quiet down as they mature.

What if my cat leaps/scratches at your windows?

37 This is often seen in an active cat that is trying to express predatory or play behavior towards movement that he sees outdoors. This may be birds, other animals, or even insects in the window. (Some cats respond to lights and shadows in the same way.) The cat is probably feeling some frustration at not being able to express his instincts sufficiently at other times.

Action: Two or three times a day, set up play times when your cat can hunt and pounce on toys you are manipulating or which are dangling from doorways or stairs. A young active cat living indoors may benefit considerably from having access to a specially made cat enclosure in your yard. This will provide him with more stimulation and good exercise while climbing up ramps and trunks.

Left and above: Even a house cat instinctively wants to hunt and pounce. Without appropriate opportunities, he'll find other ways to express himself.

What if my cat won't stay off the kitchen surfaces?

38 Many people find it distasteful to have their cats walking on their kitchen surfaces or dining room table, because a cat also spends his time walking around yards, using his paws to cover his feces, and then entering the home. Being consistent and never encouraging cats to jump up is important from the day you bring them home. Don't leave food on the counter, or jumping up will be worthwhile for the cat. Sticky tape (positioned sticky side up) or foil is a useful deterrent because cats hate sticky or shiny, crinkly surfaces. Use this whenever you are not there to supervise, such as at night, so that your cat learns that being up on the counter is always unpleasant. It can be useful to apply the tape to a plywood board or a plastic tablecloth that can be placed on and taken off the surfaces easily when you leave or enter the room. This will also prevent any sticky residue being deposited on your work-surface.

Cat environments must include spaces set on various levels, because cats feel more comfortable when they have high places where they can hide away. Create raised areas where your cat *is allowed* to jump up around the home. Commonly used areas include the tops of cupboards, wardrobes, shelves, or cat towers. Your cat is likely to feel comforted from having access to these places where he can relax and observe the world.

What if my cat collects small objects around the home?

39 Cats frequently carry around prey items, toys, or other objects. The reason **why** this occurs can often be determined by what they do with the items. Some cats simply bring them to their owners, some hoard them, and others create nests. Females can experience false pregnancies and have the urge to collect and create nests with items they see as kittens. This is hormone-driven, and your vet can advise you about the appropriate course of action.

Some cats will learn to get attention from their owners by carrying around personal items. They learn very quickly that owners respond to seeing a treasured item being carried away and begin to use this as a way to get attention. In a natural cat group, a mother cat or adult member will teach the young how to hunt by bringing live prey back to the nest to hunt or to allow the others to hunt. A pet cat may use toys or other items in this way if she has no access to real prey.

Hoarding playthings is not normally a serious problem. When a cat likes to play regularly, he may cache away all his toys so he can play whenever he wishes. This may be especially true in very tidy homes, where he learns that if he leaves an item, it will be gone (tidied away) when he returns. Occasionally, particular cats take a liking to valuable items or hoard obsessively, which can be a problem if he is stealing your neighbor's property!

What if my cat doesn't like to drink from his bowl?

40 If you're worried that your cat isn't taking in enough water, then contact your vet (see also Part 5 "What if?" no. 111). Some wet foods contain a high proportion of water, so if your cat eats this sort of diet, he may not be as thirsty as when he is fed dry food. However, if your cat never drinks from his bowl, it may be that he does not like its location. Ensure that it's placed in a safe, quiet place that he can get to easily. Older cats, or those with joint pain, may not want to jump up to their bowl.

Cats have a different sense of taste and smell than us. Still water can go stale very quickly, and this may put some cats off drinking. Water should be fresh, so replace it every day and more often during hot weather or if your pets are unwell. Some cats prefer drinking from a running tap, in which case a cat water fountain is a good idea because it won't waste water. This is a special type of bowl or dome in which filtered water is continually circulating. The moving water is well oxygenated and smells and tastes fresh. Plastic and ceramic bowls can quickly accumulate bacteria, so wash them daily. Plastic bowls can also retain an unpleasant plastic scent for some cats.

Check that his name-tag isn't banging against the bowl when he drinks and thus disturbing him. If there's more than one cat in the house, be prepared to provide several water bowls in different locations so that there's no conflict over resources or that one cat isn't the victim of bullying. Some cats simply prefer to drink from your garden pond or puddles. Even so, always provide fresh water indoors, too, so he has that option.

Below: Cats like fresh water and are often attracted to running or dripping taps when thirsty. They benefit from fresh-tasting, cool water, which doesn't harbor bacteria. A water fountain is a better option for daily use.

Below: Cats are often given cow's milk to drink, but many have a digestive intolerance to it. Fresh water is a much healthier option and will make your cat feel better, too.

What if my cat won't eat from his bowl?

41

Does your cat still have an appetite, or is he having trouble eating? Loss of appetite can be a sign of a medical problem, so refer to Part 5 "What if?" nos.128 and 131 in the first instance, because veterinary help may be required.

If the problem is a behavioral issue, you need to question some features about the bowl as mentioned in "What if?" no. 40. Is the bowl too deep to lean into, is his collar or name tag banging against the metal bowl, or is it emitting an unappealing plastic smell. The position of the bowl is also important. If your cat is anxious or new to the home, he may not want to eat from the bowl if it is too close to people or it's positioned in a busy area of the home or near his litter box. Cats like to feel safe while eating, so consider this when placing dishes.

Competition from other cats in the household may also be a deterrent. Even when no obvious conflict is apparent, there may be underlying tension, which means one cat will not eat around another. Video your cats while they are eating, because the footage may give you a clue as to what is going on, or will at least help your behaviorist make an accurate diagnosis. If you have had to medicate your cat by putting powder or tablets in his food, that experience may have been distasteful and so is causing him to shy away from his food bowl. If you have given him a tablet while he was eating from his bowl, then he may have developed an aversion to this area. In this case, change the position and the type of bowl and be prepared to add something very tempting into the food. Gradually move it back to the original position when he's eating happily again.

Above: *Reluctance to eat from a bowl may be a sign of a health problem or evidence of some kind of behavioral issue.*

What if my cat only likes certain foods?

42

Cats are renowned for being fussy eaters and for liking variety in their diet. Stick to specially made cat food unless you want to prepare meat or fish to supplement the occasional meal. Don't be made to feel guilty by those meows and feline glares. New cats should be kept on their previous diets and slowly changed onto your preferred brand of food as they relax into the routine of their new home. Cats don't need to be fed large amounts of food in one go. Small, regular meals are far more natural, and you can add variety in the flavors you offer him.

Make sure that what you are feeding is suitable for cats, and never try to feed your cat a vegetarian diet. If this is a sudden change, then talk to your vet about possible health causes, including dental problems which can result in a preference for soft foods or smaller kibbles that don't require hard chewing. Remember that stress can cause a cat to change his eating habits, so study his situation carefully; if he's showing any other signs of stress, then seek help from a cat behaviorist to solve the problem before his condition deteriorates.

What if my cat meows constantly for food?

43

Demands for food are thought to be one of the main reasons for cats becoming obese. Owners often respond to plaintive meowing by thinking that the cat is hungry. If he does seem desperately hungry, then take him for a veterinary examination to rule out any possible hormonal disorders. Your vet will also be able to advise you about providing a correct diet that provides the right amount of calories while also making your cat feel satisfied and full.

As long as your cat is healthy and has access to an appropriate amount of food each day, it's likely that he's simply learned to be demanding. Cats quickly learn that meowing results in their owner turning their focus upon them and providing tasty food or treats. Once your cat has learned that being vocal results in attention and

the provision of food, he's likely to try out his meow more often, at any time of day or night, especially when the house is quiet and there are few other distractions.

To overcome any learned vocalization problems, it's essential that every member of the household agree to ignore the demands. At first your cat will simply try harder to get his way by making even more noise. This is totally normal and is known by behaviorists as the "extinction process" (see Part 1, page 29). Stock up on earplugs to ensure you can resist responding to your cat's demands, even during the night. If the extra effort gets him no reward (such as a meal or your attention), then he'll stop wasting his energy.

As soon as he's quiet you must make the effort to give him attention and meals. If you respond to the increased noise and demands, the problem will only become much worse. Your cat will simply learn to meow louder and longer to get his meals from then on.

Action: Try to respond by playing games instead so your cat is more active but still happy. Create activity feeders that require effort and dexterity before your cat can access the food treats. These will use up time and energy, as well as involving more of your cat's natural predatory instincts, so they are more satisfying to him.

This process of changing your cat's vocal demands will take a varying amount of time, depending on your cat's natural tendencies and how long he's been rewarded for being vocal. If you have a naturally vocal breed like a Siamese, then you will need to accept that total silence isn't realistic. If your cat's reaching old age and suddenly begins meowing lots or seems constantly hungry or thirsty, then ***do seek veterinary advice.***

right: Cats quickly [lear]n to repeat any [beh]avior that brings [rew]ards. Owners respond [to t]heir kitten's mews, and [t]he habit continues to [gro]w. Meowing is often [i]nterpreted as a [dem]and for food when in [reali]ty it can have many [vari]ed meanings.

What if my cat takes food out of his bowl?

44 Many cats will take a piece of food out of their bowl, move it to another location, and consume it there. Members of the small cat family are solitary hunters by nature, and they are designed to catch, kill, and consume small prey alone. Though some can cope, others cannot relax when several cats share from one bowl at the same time. Try offering separate bowls for each cat, possibly in different places. Alternatively, giving larger food morsels that take time to tear apart can result in a cat taking the food away somewhere private to enjoy. Both are natural feline responses.

What if my cat sheds hair on the furniture or bed?

45 It's a simple fact of life that cats shed hair, and this will get on whatever chair or bed they sleep on. Grooming your cat regularly will reduce the amount of loose hair that is shed around your home. Begin grooming your cat from an early age, even if he has a short coat. Short grooming sessions with appropriate brushes and combs should be linked to tasty tidbits. Hair can be removed from furniture by using specially made sticky rollers. Place blankets over the spots where you allow your cat to sleep, because this will catch most of the hair. Some hair being shed is part of the process of living with a cat, and you must accept it. However, if your cat suddenly starts shedding copious amounts of hair and seems lethargic or his behavior has changed in some other way, then consult your veterinarian.

Left: Cats are attracted to the comfort of c furniture and can't help shedding some hair on the upholstery or bed linen as they while away the hours in slumber.

What if my cat won't sleep in the bed we bought him?

46 Matching bedding may not be as attractive to cats as it is to humans. Cats will often choose places where they feel secure to sleep, so try to place the new bed as close to th area as possible. Cats often prefer raised areas rather than beds at ground level, so it makes sense to position cat beds on top of cupboards where they can jump up or to provide radiator beds (fleece beds that hang from a radiator) where your cat can be off the ground *and* enjoy the warmth. Plac your cat's favorite blanket on the new bed as a way of introducing his own smells to the new material. Once he is using it, his scent will transfer to it properly. Never force him to use the bed. Simply show him the area and offer praise and tidbits while he is in it. When he leaves the bed, stop offering rewards so he will build a positive association with being in it.

What if my cat likes to sleep on our bed?

47 Being close to you in such a warm and cozy place is a dream for most pet cats. If they are encouraged at all, then this is likely to become a habit. Your familiar scent will comfort them, and the bed is likely to be free for their use during the daytime. If you dislike having your cat on the bed, you should remember never to encourage him and to provide him with an alternative resting area and praise him for using it. Always close bedroom doors to keep him out when unsupervised.

What if my cat won't play with the toys I bought?

48 Cats like smell, movement, texture, and sound, so make sure that the toys you offer can provide for all desires. Offer a range of toys so that your cat has something to interest him, no matter what his mood may be. Cats can be extremely picky over their choice of activity, so you will also get to know what his preferences are. If he has never been much of a player or is nervous, then you will have to tempt him slowly to join in the games. Some cats feel more confident playing without any human presence, whereas others seem to prefer interactive games.

Action: It's a good idea to create several small play boxes filled with various toys. Rotate the boxes on a weekly basis, making sure that your cat has items left to occupy him at all times. Cats can get bored seeing the same items day after day, so this should help to keep him excited. However, you may want to leave his favorite toy out all the time.

Always think carefully before giving your cat something to play with, because some objects can be very dangerous. Very small items may be ingested and cause intestinal blockages, so avoid tiny balls, strings, ribbons, and rubber bands. ▶

elow: A cat may play h the simplest toy and stratingly ignore our re expensive gifts!

Specially made cat toys will appeal to different characters. Ping pong balls with holes, balls with bells, small fur "mice," feathered toys, cat wands, the kitty kong (a rubber toy that can have treats hidden inside), and catnip creatures will attract cats, depending on their mood. Some toys will encourage independent play, whereas others do require you to be part of the game. It's a good idea to have a selection of both types. Think carefully about where you place the toys; cats love discovering items for themselves, although ball that rolls away under a sofa may simply cause frustration. Placing plastic balls in a hallway or in an empty bath for the cat to chase around can provide fantastic fun.

Homemade toys can also be lots of fun for your cat, so entertain him by making items to catch his attention. Popular versions involve toys that encourage food foraging and hunting behaviors. Boxes containing desirable treats can have holes cut into the sides so your cat is tempted to reach inside with his paws to grab the tidbits. A plastic bottle can also be adapted by making several holes in it and then filling it with dry kibble that drops out as your cat bats it about. Some cats may need to begin with a bottle with larger holes and gradually progress to more demanding versions over time.

Above: Small play items allow your cat to practice using his physical agility and precisely tune his movements. Having an outlet for his predatory instincts is important in order to avoid frustration that could lead to the development of problem behaviors.

Strings tied securely to feathers, woollen pompoms, or squeaky toys can be engaging for active hunters. You can either be part of the game by manipulating them, or they can be hung around your home to tempt your cat to leap and stretch. Cardboard tubes can be stuffed with paper and treats so your cat has to work to pull them apart to access the food. Laser pens have become popular for playtime with cats. You shine a narrow beam of light on the floor to attract the cat's attention and then wave the beam around as the cat attempts to catch it. However, because the cat can never catch his "prey," it can result in extreme frustration in some cats. A possible solution to this is to play with the light and then end the game by "landing" the light on a favored toy that can be "caught" (and the light turned off). This is a much more satisfying result for your cat, who feels that his attempts have been successful.

Cats may take time before they play properly with a new toy, so don't be immediately disheartened if he seems to reject your efforts. Always use common sense when making toys and leaving your cat alone with any item that might get tangled around his neck or choke him.

What if my cat won't use the new kitty door?

49

Cats can be cautious about new routines. Unless he's experienced and learned about using a kitty door while he was very young, it's likely to take a little time for him to build up his confidence to use it. Cats can learn by observation, so another cat who uses your kitty door may help to encourage him.

If your cat is worried about using the door because he's afraid of the outdoors, then refer to Part 4 "What if?" no. 108. He may be too scared to use the door because he has experienced an ambush from other cats or even your dog. This insecurity will have to be addressed before he will summon up sufficient courage to use the door normally. (See also Part 4 "What ifs?" nos. 91 and 92.)

Action: Securely prop the door flap open so your cat can see through the opening. Lure him through from the opposite side by calling and offering his favorite tidbit (or rattling his kibble box if that's the sound he loves most). After lots of practice, gradually lower the flap until he gets used to pushing against it. Check that the flap moves easily when he tries to push through.

Do make sure that the mechanisms of an electric or magnetic door are working correctly so that your cat doesn't get stuck, isn't frightened by it slamming behind him, or doesn't fail constantly when he tries to get out because the door does not open. This would all be counter-productive.

What if my cat is determined to lick plastic objects?

50 This odd behavior has several possible explanations. Some theories propose that the cat is detecting an odor or taste from the plastic, others suggest that the texture is appealing, while some argue that the behavior is another type of compulsive disorder like pica (chewing inedible material) or wool-sucking (see "What ifs?" nos. 32 and 33). It's always advisable to distract your cat from this activity and encourage him to perform more acceptable and functional behaviors, such as playing games, manipulating activity feeders, or being petted by his owners.

Right: Keep plastic bags out of reach if your cat tends to chew. Pieces can easily be ingested and cause intestinal blockages.

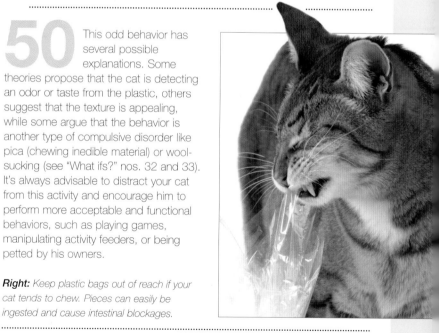

What if my cat likes to lick photographs?

51 Cats can be attracted to the ink on photographs and may lick them, removing parts of the picture. ***This is extremely dangerous because the inks are poisonous*** to cats. Always frame photos securely behind glass or keep them out of your cat's reach. If you discover or suspect that your cat has been licking photographs, then you should contact your veterinarian for advice.

67

What if my cat hides under the bed?

52 Nervous cats may retreat to safe places if they feel threatened. Often they will hide when visitors enter the home and come out again when they leave. This is a natural feline response if a cat doesn't feel comfortable around people. Cats that have come from a rescue home, had very limited human contact, or been cruelly treated may have ingrained fears, and their attempts to avoid contact with people are understandable. It's vital that these cats have access to a safe hiding place. Never try to force your cat to come out to face people. If your cat has another fear, perhaps of another animal or of an activity within your home, then you will need to address this situation, although your cat may feel perfectly safe under the bed at these times and the habit doesn't necessarily have to be viewed as a problem.

New cats will often hide and only venture outside during quiet times. As the cat familiarizes himself with his environment and finds other safe places, he'll normally increase the time he spends out of hiding. If you have a very busy, noisy household, then it's worth considering the suitability of a very nervous cat as your pet.

Action:

- Entice your cat out by leaving tasty tidbits or his dinner for him to find. Initially leave them near his hiding place, and very gradually draw him further out.
- Do not try to pet/approach/talk to/look at your cat when he first comes out. He needs to feel as a safe as possible and may feel threatened if you attempt some form of interaction too soon. When he begins to relax speak in quiet, soothing tones.
- When your cat is comfortable enough to enter a room with you, allow him to approach you in his own time. Leave tasty tidbits for him to find as he investigates the area.
- Set up a litter box nearby so your cat is not forced to eliminate in his hiding place—this will only cause further stress to you both. Create further hiding places by making space on shelves, behind chairs, and inside boxes placed around your home so that your cat can feel safe while watching the goings on in the house.
- Never allow your children, or anything else that scares your cat, to approach his safe hiding place. When he does come out, he must be allowed to approach and investigate in his own time, no matter how slow that may be.

What if my cat tries to escape outside?

53 Some cats are attracted to the outdoors and all of its exciting areas. If you have a house cat who has had experience of the outdoors and learned how stimulating the outside world can be, then he may feel frustrated at not being able to get outside again. These types of cat benefit from having access at least to a cat enclosure in the yard. Even a small lean-to shed that your cat can enter

through a window can help in the provision of sufficient environmental enrichment. You'll need to create more interesting areas within the home as well, such as with play stations, toys, and new sleeping areas. Encourage your cat to use up some energy by focusing on working tidbits out of toys or stalking feathers on cat wands. Make sure that everyone knows to be careful when opening the outside door so that your cat does not rush out past you.

Other "escape artist" cats may be trying to get away from something that is frightening them in the home. This could be numerous things, such as other cats, other pets, children, or loud noises. Try to identify what makes your cat feel nervous and address this problem, and his need to escape will be reduced. Using a pheromone diffuser (see page 30) may help to reduce his stress while you make the required changes.

Above: Cats are escape artists who can get out of the smallest window, scale the most unlikely walls, and even take advantage of temporary scaffolding, so owners must be alert.

What if my cat knocks ornaments off the fireplace?

54 Inquisitive cats have been the downfall of many treasured items. Cats naturally want to climb and jump, so provide him with areas where he can do this safely. Discourage him from climbing on forbidden areas by temporarily arranging double-sided sticky-tape or small bowls of citrus peelings at the edge. This will deter him from jumping onto the area, because cats hate sticky sensations on their feet and dislike the smell of citrus or pepper. Stabilize your ornaments by using strong sticky-tack, and put more precious ornaments safely in a cabinet.

Satisfy your cat's natural urge to climb by providing appropriate high areas and tall cat climbing stands within your home. Always remember that a cat's environment involves both horizontal and vertical space, so try to make both dimensions interesting for him.

ar right: A broken vase . upsetting to the home . ner, but accidents can . o be dangerous to your . t, who could be cut or . ay ingest small fragments . glass or china.

What if my cat is scared of the vacuum cleaner?

55 It's quite natural for a cat to fear something as noisy and unusual as a vacuum cleaner. However, it's more likely to occur if the cat had little experience of household noises as a kitten or if he has had an unpleasant experience. It's possible to reduce your cat's stress while you clean by desensitising him to the sound and sight of the vacuum cleaner. Never force him to remain in the room or move the vacuum cleaner close to him. Many cats are most comfortable if they can make their own way out of the room, so make sure the door is le open. The option to remain in the room should be available, and your cat is most likely to feel happy if he can sit high up and watch in safety.

If your cat is very frightened, you can desensitize him to the sounds b playing a sound effects CD very quietly and slowly getting him accustomed to it as you gradually increase the volume. Other cats are able to cope if the vacuum cleaner is turned on in another part of the home with the doors closed in between. During these times you should play games or offer your cat his favorite meal so that he feels happy and associate this sensation with the background noise.

What if my cat goes crazy over some plants?

56 It's likely that these plants are from the plant family *Nepeta,* which includes all varieties of catnip or catmint. When crushed or damaged, these plants emit scents that stimulate your cat and cause him to display seemingly ecstatic responses, such as rubbing, rolling, leaping, and purring. The chemical he is responding to is called **nepetalactone**. The majority of cats seem to respond to some degree to catnip, though the level of response is inherited. Very young or old cats are less likely to react to catnip. After th initial energized reaction he will begin to calm down. The next time he encounters catnip he will react once again. It's a grea addition to cat toys or a cat garden, so try sowing seeds and creating more plants for him to enjoy.

What if my cat kneads on the cushions or on me?

57 Many cats will engage in kneading actions when they are settling down or are particularly comfortable and warm. Thi behavior's original purpose was to keep milk flowing while the kitten fed from his mother. You may also notice him purring and drooling or sucking while he does this. Kittens who are not weaned properly from their mother—perhaps as a result of being rejected by the queen, hand-reared, or re-homed too early—often display this kitten behaviour as adult cats. Occasionally females in heat will knead or paddle more often than normal, and so it's thought that it may also be a sexual behavior.

If you dislike this behavior you can gently move your cat to a cushion or stuffed toy that you are happy to have kneaded in this way. The action can involve the extension and retraction of claws, which can be particularly uncomfortable on a human lap. As soon as your cat begins this, gently move him off you. Don't punish him, because this is a natural response and he will feel distressed and confused if he is admonished for it. Try to view the behavior as a sign that your cat is comfortable and content.

ove: Happy kittens knead encourage milk flow.

hat if my cat grooms until he has bald patches?

58 Overgrooming can be an indication of a parasite problem or localized pain, so your cat should be checked over by your vet as soon as possible (see also Part 5, "What if" no. 150). Excessive grooming can also indicate a high degree of stress caused by something in his environment or by the lack of other suitable stimulation. Grooming is often used by cats as a way to reduce tension and help calm themselves. If the cat is under too much stress or has little else to occupy himself, he may begin to use grooming as a way to cope with daily life. Excessive grooming for nonmedical reasons should be taken as a sign that something in your cat's world is amiss. It's more serious than a spoiled coat and excessive hair balls. You need to assess his living arrangements, identify what could be causing him such distress, and make changes that improve the situation.

If your cat is extremely distressed or has been overgrooming for a very long time, then occasionally it's necessary to seek advice regarding anti-anxiety medication. However, in these cases you should seek advice from a behavioral specialist first, who will help you to address the environmental or social problems that are causing your cat to feel stressed. If you do not do this, the problem is likely to recur.

bove: Cats naturally like keep themselves clean nd will regularly groom roughout the day.

ight: If your cat is hard distract while he's rooming or there are ald or thinning patches ppearing, then seek dvice from your vet.

MISHAPS AND PROBLEMS DURING SOCIAL INTERACTIONS

PART 3

CONTENTS

What if my cat . . .

INTRODUCTION

Cats may have become the most popular domestic pet, but many problems can occur while they are interacting with their owners or with other pets in the home. These issues can be significant, especially those involving cat bites or scratches, which can transmit infections and should always be taken seriously. If your cat is very distressed during any encounter, then it's best to seek behavioral advice so that your own situation can be analyzed and a program devised for you.

What if my cat bites or scratches when I'm petting him?

Far right: Look out for lowered ears, bristling hair, or twitching tails to warn of a pending reaction.

59 Some cats love sitting on your lap, whereas others avoid being handled. Each cat has his own tolerance level. Genetics play a part in this, but early socialization is also very important in the development of a cat's temperament. If your cat didn't have enough gentle handling as a small kitten, it's likely that he could feel anxious about being handled as an adult.

If your cat is nervous around people, you will have to start to build up his confidence slowly. Quiet, calm and patient people are best suited to this type of cat, so if you have a very busy household, or perhaps energetic young children, it may be harder to reduce your cat's anxiety.

Never force your cat to remain on your lap. By letting him go when he feels he has had enough, he will be more likely to feel confident enough, to approach you again later. If he chooses to come and sit with you, avoid the temptation to pet him too vigorously. A gentle touch linked to something your pet really loves, such as a tasty tidbit, will start to encourage him to spend time with you. Never overwhelm him with too much petting at once, or he may start to avoid you completely.

Alternatively, some very confident cats will seek out petting by a person but become over-aroused by vigorous petting. Their excitement results in aggressive play behavior after a few minutes. Often these cats were encouraged to play roughly as kittens when the damage they could cause was minimal.

Avoid the temptation to pet your cat continuously. Stroke him briefly and then let him settle down again. Watch his body language, because any signs of restlessness may indicate that he is becoming irritated.

Slow, gentle petting is preferable to quick, wiggly fingers that may trigger play-biting. Don't try to pet him immediately after excitable games, because it takes time for cats to calm down.

Don't shout or smack him, because this will only make him more likely to be aggressive toward you next time. Try to be aware of your cat's reactions even when you are distracted by the TV or are chatting on the phone.

If your cat has always enjoyed being petted without any problem and has suddenly changed his behavior, then it's vital to ask your vet to examine him. Accidents and illness can both result in pain or sensitivity that needs to be addressed urgently. **Remember to seek medical advice if you are bitten or scratched**, because cats may transmit serious infections.

above: Kittens can learn to see hands as playthings, which can lead to unwanted predatory behavior.
above top: Fingers are particularly vulnerable, so stroke slowly and calmly.

right: After a cat has reacted, he will need time to relax before you attempt other petting.

What if my cat causes allergies?

60

Most people who react to cats are often responding to dander, which is composed of skin flakes and dried saliva (from when the cat washes himself) as well as secretions from glands. This is why people can still react toward hairless cats and non shedding pets. Allergies are very personal and vary between one person a the next. Some people find that short-haired cats cause them less reactior whereas others may react differently to very similar cats. If an allergy is not extreme, some people find that over time they desensitize to their pet. The pleasure gained from owning a cat often outweighs the inconvenience of having a minor allergy. It's estimated that about a third of cat-allergy suffere continue to share their lives with feline companions.

Action: Basic suggestions to try before panicking and re-homing your cat are

✔ Keep him out of your bedroom, and most certainly off your bed.
✔ High-efficiency air purifiers around the home can help by removing any particles in the air.
✔ Clean and vacuum regularly (using a vacuum with powerful filter). Look for machines that have a high-efficiency particulate air (HEPA) filter Where possible, avoid buying carpets and soft furnishings which catch and retain the allergens for years.
✔ Groom your cat daily so there is less buildup of dander. If he allows it, c this outdoors or in a well-vented area in order to prevent an extreme reaction as you disturb the dander. Grooming can also include wipir him down with cloths to remove more dander. Accustom your ca gradually to all this handling, and make sure he feels comfortable and relaxed.
✔ Place blankets over the areas where your cat sleeps most and exchange and wash these regularly. This should prevent the buildup of hair and skin particles on your furniture.
✔ Bear in mind that allergies are cumulative; they build up over time, so regular cleaning an avoiding all the other things to which you are reactive will also help to reduce the likelihood of your cat triggering your allergies.

Above: *An allergy to cats can range from a slight sniffle to much more serious breathing difficulties requiring medical treatment.*

What if my cat suddenly leaps up during petting and becomes very agitated?

61

If your cat is normally happy to be handled but then becom irritable, then "What if?" no. 59 may answer your query.

However, if your cat leaps off your lap and you also notice the skin on his back rippling, then it's likely that he is experiencing a conditic called **Feline Hyperesthesia Syndrome**. This is when the skin seems to r or twitch uncontrollably. It seems to be triggered by petting and stroking, among other things, but the true cause is still unclear. Some breeds are mc susceptible to this condition than others, and it seems to create discomfort which explains why they suddenly leap away from you to stop you from stroking them. Breeds like the Siamese, Burmese, and Abyssinian seem to

present with this problem slightly more than others but it's by no means restricted to pedigree cats. Since this condition can result from a health problem, it's worth taking your cat to the vet for a thorough physical examination (see also Part 5). If the all-clear is given by the vet, then you may have to address any environmental stresses that your cat may be experiencing, because anxiety is thought to be linked to the condition. Be especially aware when you are petting your cat, and stop if he shows any signs of becoming sensitive.

What if my cat starts fighting my other cat?

62 Cat fights are frightening and a real concern for owners. If your cats have lived happily together for a long time and have only just started fighting, then you need to ask your vet to check both cats over to determine any possible medical reasons for bad temper. If that does not reveal any problems, then you will need to consider what changes have occurred in the household recently that may have upset the social balance. These can include moving, the arrival of new people, people leaving the home, or changes in the area.

First you need to be honest about how well the cats were bonded before this occurred. Cats are specialists at overt aggression, which means you may have missed the early signs that can include stares or avoidance behavior. The mere fact of co-habitation is not enough to say they were close. Did the cats regularly groom one another or rub along each other when greeting, and could they be found curled up tightly together during naps? If so, then they probably did have a good relationship. If not, then they probably only tolerated one another and something has occurred to tip the balance. If they were strongly bonded, then it's likely that you'll be able to identify an event that changed this bond.

Top: Many inherited conditions like feline hyperaesthesia are still not fully understood.

Below: Maturing cats might fight over access to important resources such as territory, sleeping areas, mates, food, water, and even their owner's attention.

If either cat is reaching maturity, then competition for resources may be occurring. Aggression between maturing male cats is common, and you may see lots of hissing and growling. In a natural cat group this is the time when the young males move on to find groups of their own. Females can also display aggression during maturation. Castration and spaying reduce this type of aggression problem significantly. Older cats may have problems, because elderly individuals may be less able to interact normally with others and fighting can occur. ▶

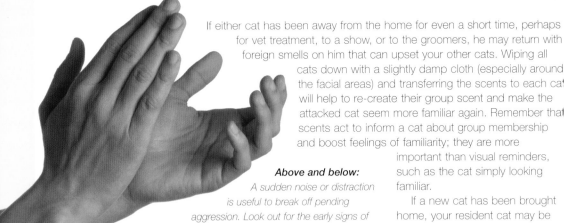

If either cat has been away from the home for even a short time, perhaps for vet treatment, to a show, or to the groomers, he may return with foreign smells on him that can upset your other cats. Wiping all cats down with a slightly damp cloth (especially around the facial areas) and transferring the scents to each cat will help to re-create their group scent and make the attacked cat seem more familiar again. Remember that scents act to inform a cat about group membership and boost feelings of familiarity; they are more important than visual reminders, such as the cat simply looking familiar.

Above and below:

A sudden noise or distraction is useful to break off pending aggression. Look out for the early signs of tension to forestall an actual fight.

If a new cat has been brought home, your resident cat may be displaying territorial aggression toward this newcomer. Refer to "What if?" no. 79 for introduction suggestions.

Action: Though there are several causes for aggression, there are some sensible actions you can take now. Don't let the cats fight it out. This does not resolve conflict in cats and will result in more aggression in the future. Address any of the recent changes that you can and make provisions for each cat. If the aggression is severe, you may need to separate them and re-introduce them very carefully over many sessions. Create additional escape routes and more hiding places for the attacked cat, provide separate feeding and watering stations, more litter boxes, and routes to the outdoors. Using a pheromone diffuser, available from your vet, can also help to soothe ruffled tempers.

If you spot the aggressor cat threatening the other, perhaps with a glaring stare, break off the incident by clapping or creating another distracting noise. Then quickly place something between the cats if possible. As always, **never use punishment** in an attempt to solve feline aggression problems. Don't try to pull the cats apart, because you will probably get injured.

What if my cat fights with our neighbor's cat?

63

It's very common for clashes between neighboring cats to occur. This is normally due to the fact that the territories are unnaturally close together. Both cats feel that the other is invading and, because of their owner's working hours, may find themselves out at similar times and unable to avoid one another. Sometimes communicating with the other owner can be useful, because neither of you wants extra trips to the vet to treat bite abscesses brought about through fighting. Remain calm and don't take the situation too personally; fighting neighbors won't help the situation one bit! You need to work together. If

relations are good, then one simple solution is to come to an agreement with your neighbor about **time sharing**, because this is how cats would normally avoid conflict. Agree to let each cat out at certain times and to keep them in at other times.

Action: When cats will be out at the same time, then you should create more areas in your own yard where your cat can feel safe. Cats do accept that others may be in their area but dislike having to come face to face with them because their lack of ability to perform submissive displays means that their encounters normally result in a fight. Providing more ways for your cat to traverse the property will make it less likely that the cats will find themselves eye to eye as each goes about his business. Place plant pots, benches, bushes, walkways, and perches between trees or along fences to provide your cat with more options within this environment for hiding or avoiding the other cat. Also create a latrine area so your cat doesn't have to travel into other properties to relieve himself: a sheltered area with some slightly soiled litter, sand, or shavings may entice him to use it. If your cat is clearly the main aggressor, then it can help to let others know he is around by attaching a couple of bells to his collar to provide some advance warning, which will allow other cats to move out of his way.

Above: If possible, let the cats out at different times to prevent confrontations.

Below: Meeting a rival cat often leads to aggression.

What if my cat grooms my hair?

64 Social grooming, or allogrooming, occurs between socially compatible cats. It's even estimated that an adult cat living with a companion can spend up to half his waking time engaging in grooming with that cat. Doing so builds bonds and establishes group identity. If your cat is grooming you, then he obviously feels relaxed and contented. Young kittens often do this to their owners, but it's often a good idea to limit this habit because the cat can begin to try it more often and can actually begin to chew the hair, too, which is less acceptable to most owners.

Left: *Close contact and transference of group scents helps to maintain strong relationships. If your cat is obsessive about licking and chewing hair, you should provide distractions and seek advice.*

What if my cat follows me everywhere?

65 Cats can become over-attached to their owners. This is often when they are insecure or have little else to distract them. Make sure that you are not responding in a way which encourages this behavior, such as talking to him, petting him, or offering food. These things should obviously be provided, but not while your cat is behaving in this needy manner.

Action: Spend time discovering what games your cat likes, and arrange it so that he starts playing by himself. Hanging furry toys or feathers from doorjambs or stairs can be enticing, as can toys that wiggle and jiggle around randomly when patted with a paw. Hiding small treats or bowls of food around the home can also be a great way of keeping your cat busy while he searches for them. If your cat seems to be nervous when alone, then try to identify what is causing the anxiety. Help to make him feel safe by creating new hiding places, perhaps by clearing a space on shelves or cupboards where he can sit and watch the world. If there are other pets or even young children in the home, then make sure that your cat feels safe when left alone with them. Sometimes an owner's being nearby provides security and protection from exuberant dogs or children or inhibits another pet from attacking or threatening the cat.

What if my cat won't let me pick him up?

66 If your cat suddenly becomes aggressive or fearful when you try to lift him up but was happy previously, then you need to get him carefully into the cat-carrier and visit your vet, who can check for injury (see also Part 5, "What if?" no. 121).

Tolerance of various types of handling by people is learned when the cat is very young. If the cat was lifted in a way that caused discomfort or did not get used to gentle restriction by his owner, then he is likely to resist future lifting. Negative associations may also be made if you had to lift him to administer medical treatment at any point. Remember that when lifting a cat you should support his weight and avoid lifting him up or down too quickly. Always question whether the cat actually needs to be lifted up. Lifting simply because a child wants to or you feel like it are not good enough reasons.

Cats that are normally comfortable when being handled and petted can gently be taught to accept being held, and this can be helpful in emergencies. Begin by briefly holding your cat while you are sitting. Offer him a tasty treat for allowing this. Build up slowly until you can hold him briefly before giving him his reward. (Though don't use lifting and restraint if he's trying to get to his dinner, because this will annoy him.) The rule should be lift, then offer rewards immediately. Never lean over him to pick him up, because he may feel startled, and don't pick him up under his armpits or with his full weight on his stomach. It's better to crouch next to him and lift from there or to lure him up onto a higher surface where you can easily take hold of him. Remember to support his body with one arm along his length and to hold him close to you so he feels secure. If you need to pick him up in an emergency, then place a large towel over him and lift him up, ensuring the towel restricts his leg movements.

Many cats love being handled, but sudden avoidance might signal pain, so arrange a vet check.

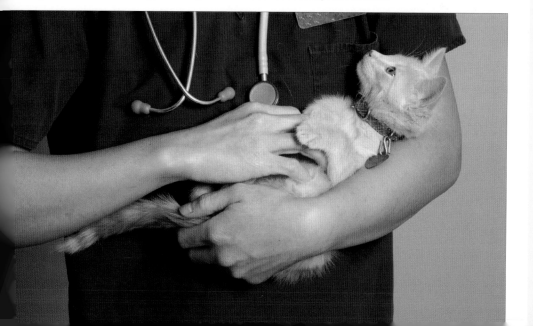

What if my cat meows during the night?

67

Many owners complain about the nocturnal activities of their cat. Cats are not truly nocturnal, though most will have active times during the night. During this time they may seek out social interaction with you. Most cats learn early on in their lives that meowing is a reliable way to gain attention from people. They have no understanding of socially appropriate times for meowing and are not deliberately trying to prevent you from getting a good night's sleep.

The most important advice for dealing with this undesirable habit is not to respond to it. As discussed in Part 1, cats learn by experience; if they do something and it works, then they will continue to do it. Meowing will continue if they get interaction from you. Since this is easier said than done at 3 A.M., there are some other routines that you can put in place to make your nights more peaceful.

Action:

- Ensure that your cat has plenty of activities and items to keep him entertained when he wakes. These can include toys left out to play with, morsels of his food for him to search for, and comfy cat beds in various places so he can swap during the night.
- Keep earplugs by your bed, and use them until the problem resolves. Put these away during the day, because cats will often play with—and consume—earplugs.
- Exercise and stimulation during the day are useful so that he does not wake up ready and charged up for action in the night.
- Your cat will need access to a latrine area during the night; if he cannot go outside, then provide a litter tray so he does not have to meow to be let out. If your cat is elderly and has begun meowing during the night, please refer to Part 6.

What if my cat wants me to play in the middle of the night?

68

Cats naturally have different sleeping and waking patterns from people and are often active during the night, much to the chagrin of their owners. (Please refer to "What ifs?" nos. 67, 159 and 160 for more information about related problems.) Make sure your cat has sufficient play and stimulation during the day. See also the section on toys and games for more ideas about keeping him occupied ("What if?" no. 48).

Far right: Cats are not truly nocturnal; instead, they have several active periods during the night and day when they might want to play.

What if my cat jumps out and claws me?

69

Predatory behavior can be directed toward owners, other family members, or even visitors. This often happens when the person walks past the cat and hasn't noticed him hiding and waiting for this opportunity. The main attack is normally focused on the ankles and feet and can involve biting and clawing. It can be extremely shocking and upsetting for owners and worrying when it's directed toward children.

Cats have an absolute need to express the full range of natural feline activities. Pet cats often don't get this opportunity when they get their food put into a bowl each day and have limited play/hunting opportunities. In a natural situation, a cat would get to search for prey, hunt it down, capture it, and kill and consume it. A pet cat often only gets to do the last part of the sequence when his owner puts the bowl of food down each day. To be completely satisfied, he needs to perform the other parts of his natural urges too. This is when he begins to "hunt" other items or even people. Single cats often present with this more often, because they have less play interaction. Another situation where this occurs is when a kitten has been played with and encouraged to chase after feet. The kitten learns that feet are something that predatory and play behaviors can be focused upon.

Action: It's important to change the circumstances so your cat does not need to perform this game. Provide alternative games, and if your cat is pouncing on you regularly, it helps to temporarily protect yourself with stout boots or similar ankle and leg protection. When your cat pounces, don't leap away squealing. By quietly **standing still**, you make this game very boring for your cat. If you see your cat getting ready to pounce (perhaps he is crouched behind an item), tell him firmly "**No**" and stop moving. When he relaxes you can continue to walk past; now praise him and give him another game to play. Once he has stopped practicing this game, he will start to focus more on the other activities you have introduced.

Note: Keep your cat's nails trimmed to reduce the damage they cause. It's easiest to get a young kitten used to having its nails trimmed from a very early age. This is a painless procedure that you can learn to do at home.

Above: Your cat's feline instincts will be expressed in different behaviors, but the most acceptable way to satisfy his predatory desires is by playing games with toys.

What if my cat starts to flick his tail while I'm petting him?

70

This is a sign of irritation or arousal. It's best to slow or stop your petting, because he is actually sending a signal of impending aggression. Learn more about your cat's body language and its interpretation in Part 1.

Right: Understanding your cat's signals allows you to avoid interactions he dislikes.

What if my cat won't let anyone near me?

71

Sometimes a cat can begin to become aggressive if another person approaches him and his owner. Often this occurs where the cat has bonded very closely to one person, perhaps a single owner who is the main caregiver and provider of resources such as food and comfort. Often these cats have not been socialized thoroughly with a full range of people and feel some anxiety when a person approaches. Having their owner close by gives them the confidence to react, whereas when alone many of these cats will move away and avoid the person, if they can. Some cats simply decide that they don't wish to share their wonderful owner and begin to defend them from other family or friends. In this case, the cat often remains near his owner when visitors are in the home. It's common for the owner of such a cat to have accidentally reinforced the aggressive behavior by taking hold of the cat and petting or soothing him in another way when he starts to be aggressive toward another person. **This needs to stop**; your cat must learn that this is not a desirable behavior.

Action: Here are a few suggestions that you should follow to make this situation easier:

- **No reinforcing.** This means you should not pet or talk to your cat if he is behaving badly.
- Put the cat into **another area** where he doesn't have to be near visitors. This allows your visitors and the cat to relax away from one another and does not perpetuate the problem.
- **Introduce** regular visitors as described in "What if?" no. 86.
  - Provide **new safe areas** so the cat does not need to stay close by you for security.
- **Change your relationship** with your cat by interacting on your own terms. While visitors are around, he may not be able to have your full attention, so get him used to this at other times.

What if my cat won't let me groom him?

72

Although cats are normally good at keeping themselves well groomed and clean, elderly individuals and those with long hair or health problems may be unable to keep their coats in good condition. Show cats obviously need extra care to keep them in tip-top condition.

Once a cat has developed a dislike of being handled in any way, it can be a real challenge to keep on top of his care. Early socialization and handling are essential so that the cat is comfortable and relaxed enough to allow this. This means that kittens should be handled from an early age and encouraged to get used to hands-on sessions, such as grooming and ear, eye, and teeth checks. By taking the time to do this, you are reducing the stress your cat will experience later in life when these events are necessary. Early sessions should always be relaxed and positive, so go slowly, offering tasty tidbits and petting as rewards.

Regular grooming will be necessary. Soft rubber brushes are normally favored to begin with, because cats seem to enjoy the massaging sensations while the dead hair is pulled free. Those with longer coats need more time and gradual desensitization to the feelings of being combed. If your cat has a long coat that has become badly matted, then it's probably fairer to have his coat clipped off by a groomer so you can both start afresh. Without the tangles to deal with, you are more likely to be able to build up short and positive sessions and increase his tolerance to being handled.

Never try to praise or sympathize with a cat that is being fractious, because you will probably only encourage the unwanted behavior. Stay calm, try to relax, and keep tension out of your voice. It's our responsibility to teach our cats to tolerate this type of handling by people. Allogrooming (when cats groom one another) is normally a very peaceful time that works to tighten the bond between cats in the same social group. Never squeeze or grab your cat if he's uncomfortable. He will feel more stressed than ever and may retaliate and seriously hurt you in his attempts to escape.

Above: *Regular grooming is essential for long-haired and elderly cats who won't be able to maintain their coat by themselves.*

Left: *Short, pleasant grooming sessions will build up an unhappy cat's tolerance. Gentle massage techniques will aid relaxation and ease the grooming experience.*

What if my cat rubs against my legs every day?

73

Cats rub against people and items in their territory in order to spread their scent, which is secreted from sebaceous glands on their head, chin, and cheeks. Rubbing up against you in this way, or **bunting**, acts to spread their scent and refamiliarize you with the group. Cats can detect these subtle scents by using their amazing sense of smell, which is said to parallel that of dogs!

Right: A cat's friendly greeting often includes leg rubbing like this.

Above: Avoid towering over a nervous cat, and offer rewards for calmness.

What if my cat is scared of me?

74

New cats or those who have had little socialization or even a bad experience may fear people. Sometimes it's possible to improve this relationship, though many cats will remain wary and you will have to adjust your interactions to suit their characters.

When your cat approaches you, respond gently and calmly. Never chase him to get interaction, or you will increase his fear. Never allow your children to chase him either, even if your cat seems confident with them. Spend time in the areas where your cat likes to relax so that he associates you with these places; this will help increase the likelihood of your spending more time together. Forcing him to spend time in areas he dislikes, but which are convenient for you, will make your problem worse.

Be aware of your body language when interacting with your timid cat. If you bend over a nervous cat, he may feel threatened. It will help if you si on the floor with him or offer treats while he's up on the sofa or on another higher surface. Use a calm, quiet voice when interacting with your cat. Do employ sudden movements that may startle him. Time and patience will be necessary to win over your cat's trust.

What if my cat has to be introduced to our new baby?

75 Bringing a new baby home is going to change your household significantly, which is likely to stress the resident cat. Your routine is going to change, there will be strange sounds and smells, and you may be more concerned about where your cat spends his time when he is in the house.

If your cat currently sleeps in the bedroom, and you want this to stop once you bring baby home, then the earlier you institute the change, the better. If your cat is used to getting lots of attention and spending all his time on your lap, then it will be necessary to begin to distance yourself gradually during your pregnancy. Unfortunately this is often a time when cats get more attention and cuddles, especially when the woman is in the late stages of pregnancy and at home more often. It's also necessary to address changes in room use, because your cat may have always used the spare room as his own and may find himself suddenly evicted when the baby arrives.

Action: Allow your cat to see and hear babies and children as much as possible before the birth. If you don't know any that can visit your home, then use sound effects CDs to desensitize him to the noises. Allow your cat access to all the new items coming into your home, such as the crib, baby changing mats, and toys so he can familiarize himself and get over the changes before baby is added to the situation. Cats are often more curious when they don't know what is in a particular area, so allowing them to investigate frequently when it's safe makes it easier all around. Obviously you should not allow him to settle or make himself too comfortable in the baby's room if you don't want him in there later.

Take a blanket home from the hospital and allow your cat to familiarize himself with the baby's smell. If the cat experiences a sudden loss of attention while the baby is present, then he will start to make negative associations with its presence. Try to get back to a routine as close to your old one as possible, at least as far as your cat is concerned.

Never force your cat to come and see the baby. He will gradually build up his confidence to investigate. Remain relaxed when your cat does come over to say hello. Remember that cats do not wish babies any harm. They may like to cuddle up to them for warmth, but this is normally unlikely and can be easily prevented using mosquito netting over the crib or baby carriage. You can make these yourself from net material, but make sure they are fitted tightly or your cat may decide that it makes a perfect sleeping hammock! It's an urban myth that cats regularly suffocate babies. There has been only one recorded case. More often cats become fiercely protective of their new family baby. If care is taken and common sense is exercised, cats and babies can cohabit in the same house very safely.

Right: Cats and children can develop great relationships if they are given their own space and introduced carefully. Socialization with children is essential so your cat will be comfortable and confident.

Above: It's untrue that cats pose extreme danger to babies; be sensible, and they're likely to bond well.

What if my cat plays too roughly?

Far right: A kitten learns how to play through experience, so it's essential to avoid games involving your hands or feet. Encourage him to pounce on toys instead to provide relief for you and any other cats you may own.

76

Cats can be fantastic companions but when excited some tend to play a little too roughly with other cats or family members. The best way to prevent inappropriate play is **never** to allow a kitten to play with your hands instead of toys. If associations are made while he is learning about the world, then he will continue to think that hands are play items when he is an adult.

Always supervise him when he is playing with children, and ensure that they use cat wands or similar items to keep the cat away from their hands or feet. Watch your cat for signs that he is becoming aroused while playing. Direct his attention onto appropriate toys, and then praise him. Young cats do play very actively, and this can often be redirected onto large stuffed toys. Stop the game the moment he makes a mistake and focuses his play on you. He will learn that this type of game is not worth bothering with.

What if my cat won't let our other cats through the kitty door?

77

Kitty doors are a fantastic invention for owners, but while they allow your cat a sense of freedom, they can cause problems. The door is part of a cat's territory; therefore if the cats in your home are not all part of the same social group and happy to share with one another, the door may become "controlled" by one member or one group. Unfortunately, doors are very easily patrolled.

You can determine the groupings by watching your cats carefully. Those who groom one another, sleep or sit closely together, and share other resources are part of the same group. A cat who is not involved in mutual grooming or rubbing and who does not make physical contact with the others during sleeping or social times most probably forms a separate social group. Different groups can live in one home, which can make it very confusing for owners to recognize the separation.

If there is kitty door control occurring, you will need to create separate exits for each group of cats so they don't have to share one point of egress. This does take thought and commitment by owners, but owning multiple cats is a responsibility. Other options include creating a more excitin living arrangement for all the cats so they are busy and have less time to patrol the flap. Help your cat feel safe by placing plants and other screens around the door outside so your cat can approach and check for any guards in safety.

What if my cat is bored?

78

If your cat is very active and is constantly trying to get you to play or give him attention, then you will need to consider ways to enrich his life. More play opportunities, both with you and while he is alone, should be arranged. Adding complexity and interest to your cat's environment is the ideal way to relieve boredom. See "What if?" no. 48 for ideas about toys that may help to keep him entertained.

Sometimes a companion cat can satisfy a cat's requirements, but you do need to consider this very carefully, because not all cats can live together successfully, and even those that tolerate one another may not be part of the same social group. Some cats are better as single pets and can experience a great deal of stress if made to live with others in too small a space. If your cat has had a social companion in the past or is very young, then a friend may be ideal. Ensure you introduce them carefully, or you risk creating a worse situation.

Left: *An active cat might need more interaction than you can give, but don't assume he'll necessarily be happy with a new feline friend as a source of stimulation.*

Below: *A companion can satisfy a cat's desires for close social contact and more stimulation, although you must assess their characters carefully.*

What if my cat has to be introduced to our new cat?

79

Cats take great care to reduce the chances of bumping in new individuals by using scent marking and visual signals. They like to gather information about the other's character and familiarize themselves. Knowing this, it's easy to imagine how startling must be to suddenly come through the kitty door, or be carried into the livi room, and come face to face with the "new" cat. **Occasionally** immediate meetings work out; however, more often than not problems occur and ther take serious backpedalling to rectify. Success is more likely if you take you time and plan the introduction. Often cats work things out despite their owner's mistakes, but it's better to create a harmonious situation from the beginning.

Action:

1 Bring your new cat home and restrict him to one room away from your resident cat for a few days. He needs time to familiarize himself with his new surroundings and get over the stress of the move.

2 Swap scents between your cats by exchanging bedding and by wiping/grooming both with a new cloth and swapping the scents from one to the other.

3 Supervise your new cat while he explores the rest of your home. Your original cat can be allowed access to the new cat's room at this time so he can investigate. If you live by yourself, then use a cat carrier to keep one cat away from the other.

4 Allow visual contact but no physical contact by either opening the door just a crack (use a door stop to prevent it from accidentally opening too far) or by allowing them to see one another through a glass door (less effective due to lack of scent messages and possible close contact). If they are relaxed, you can encourage play by threading a string under the door and tying a feather or another interesting toy to each end. A long straw with feathers taped at the end is also useful. If the cats begin to play, then they will associate the fun with one another.

5 Reward both cats when they are in each other's vicinity. Remain calm and keep your voice steady and confident.

6 Bring the new cat out of his room for a few minutes at first. You should gradually increase this over a period of days. Never force the cats to meet one another. This will cause stress and ruin the hard work you have done.

7 **Never punish the cats by yelling or smacking** if any altercation doe occur. Both cats are likely to link this response with being in each other presence.

8 Praise your resident cat for his tolerance of the new cat, but take care t avoid soothing and petting when he is stressed or showing aggression.

9 If a clash does occur, then simply call a halt to the session and give the ca a break from one another. When they have calmed down, you can allow them to try again. If aggression does begin, it's unwise to allow them to battle it out, because an extremely frightening event will have repercussion for both cats and will reduce the chances of success the next time. Use

Above: *Group scent is important to cats, so swapping bedding may help.*

Below: *Initial clashes might occur if the new cat's introduction is rushed or if either feels threatened.*

Below: Introductions can vary immensely—some cats bond immediately, others fight. Sometimes characters can clash to the extent that living together is never possible.

noise distraction, a blanket, or a squirt of water to stop fighting, though ideally you should break off the encounter before this occurs.

10 Never rush this process. For some cats it will take several weeks or even months depending on their mutual hostility and inherent characters. If you have taken the time to choose and introduce your new cat, then a happy outcome is more likely.

What if my cat attacks my new kitten?

80 Previous social experience and innate temperament will determine how the cats react to this type of change. Cats typically take a few weeks to settle down, but owners of severely aggressive cats should seek help to reintroduce the cat and kitten properly. In this case follow the procedure described in "What if?" no. 79. Young cats are easier to introduce to a resident cat, though some are still viewed as an unwelcome intruder. You must take care to prevent the tiny kitten from becoming injured. Some minor hissing from both cats may occur, but this should diminish each day. A pen or indoor kennel can be very useful during the initial introduction. The kitten can be placed in the pen to stop him from running away when he sees your adult cat and to protect him from being chased. The cats will get used to seeing one another, and eventually the initial reactivity will decrease enough for the door of the pen to be opened and a calm meeting to occur. Initially, meetings should be supervised until the cats are comfortable in one another's presence.

If severe aggression occurs despite very careful introductions, then you may have to come to accept that your original cat is better off as a single cat and is not suited to mixing with others.

What if my cat is scared of my dog?

81

You must consider whether your cat has a good reason to be fearful. Cats can live alongside dogs, but historically cats would be prey species for canines, so there is a natural fear. If your dog chases your cat, or even simply tries to play with your cat, it still may be too much for him to cope with. If this is the case, then you need to spend time training your dog to be calm.

Keep your dog on his leash so he cannot attempt to chase the cat. Child gates can help to segregate the two animals while allowing them both to get used to one another's presence. Ensure your cat has plenty of access to high places where he can stay safely out of reach.

Your cat's early experience is vital to his ability to interact with dogs. He may never be confident in this circumstance, and you should never force him to face your dog. Over time, with the right program he should build more confidence but each cat will have different tolerance levels.

Take your time introducing pets, because rushing and causing stress will make your job much harder. Separate the animals until you are ready to start introducing and have time to focus on the plan. Initially, swap scents so they grow accustomed to each other's presence. Swap locations and/or swap scents by wiping a cloth over each and transferring the scent to the other to create a communal smell. This will help to reduce your cat's fear response, which means your dog will react less too.

If your cat has to use a kitty door to enter or exit the home, then make sure he does not have to pass by your dog each time he does so. It won't take long for him to learn to avoid using the flap and may mean you end up with other behavioral problems, such as inappropriate elimination in the house.

Above: *Any dog will seem frightening to a tiny kitten, but calm, controlled meetings should lead to raised confidence and a tolerant relationship. Never leave your pets together without there being escape routes available for your cat.*

What if my cat tries to hunt our smaller pets?

82

The natural predatory instincts of cats may be a problem in homes where small animals are also kept. In most instance the cat will simply be mesmerized and will never take the action further, but this is highly dependent on your cat's character and hunting ability.

Action: Make sure that cages and enclosures are secure and strong enough to withstand your cat is jumping onto them. Many cats will try to ge closer in order to watch the animal's movements more closely. This can be dangerous if a fish tank lid collapses or the hamster castle topples over. Do not allow small pets such as hamsters to run in their exercise ball aroun your cat. The hamster may seem safe, but he may feel extremely stressed the cat starts to hunt him or bat the exercise ball around.

As prey animals, rabbits can become very stressed when they are around cats. However, if brought up together so that they ar very familiar with one another, the situation need not be too stressfu

Far right: A cat may seem lost without his familiar companion and may need extra attention from his owners to combat feelings of loneliness.

Always provide your rabbit with safe shelter away from the threat of cat stares and pounces, and never leave small or young rabbits running freely with your cat. A rabbit may seem too large for a cat to prey upon, but some cats regularly catch young rabbits, and even failed attempts can cause a great deal of injury and distress. Do not allow small children to handle small pets while the cat is nearby, because any escapees may be caught and killed very quickly.

The welfare of the other pets in your house is very important. If your cat is very persistent, then you could use a remote alarm, which is set off when your cat gets too near to the cage. Provide your cat with plenty of other options for hunting games in other areas of the home.

What if my cat has lost his sibling?

Below: A grieving cat may call out just like a kitten will do on finding himself alone.

83 The loss of a close companion can be traumatic, and some cats certainly do seem to go through a grieving process. Other behavioral changes are likely, because the social group has changed and access to resources has also altered. Cats do seem to miss their lost companion and can spend a lot of time searching or waiting for them to return home. During this time it's helpful to try to keep your cat indoors or at least close to home to prevent him from roaming away. While your cat is adapting to the change, he may seem depressed, anxious, or clingier or quieter than normal. Some cats adjust very quickly, but others may take up to six months to fully adjust. Make sure that you encourage relaxed behavior, and don't try to compensate and change your responses in an attempt to make your cat happier again. This won't work, because your cat does not think this way, and it's actually likely to create dependency problems. It's always best to follow your normal routine.

Replacing a lost companion can be difficult. Your cat will already be going through an unsettled period, and a new cat entering the home may cause more stress and further problems. It's often easier to introduce a new cat to the home when you learn that one is ill (providing it's a noncontagious illness), because there's no other disruption for the cats at this time. It's very difficult to know how successful a new match will be. Don't try to replace a lost cat with one that simply looks similar, because your resident cat will immediately know the difference. Take your time and introduce them carefully if you decide that this is the right choice for you.

What if my cat won't share a bowl with our other cat?

84 It's not natural for all cats to share resources like food bowls. They have evolved to hunt individually. In a natural situation, some cats will choose not to come face-to-face with one another; they "time-share" resources in the territory. In a home situation, problems may easily arise due to the way resources are provided or dispersed. A confident cat may ward off other cats in the home by subtl body postures that you may miss. The other cat stays away or learns to avoid the bowl in order to prevent friction or an attack.

It's always best to provide several feeding/watering stations within you home so your cat can avoid any conflict and so each has sufficient access to food. After all, the cats may be friends, but if one has a bigger appetite than the other, it's easy to see how sharing may not be ideal.

What if my cat dislikes children?

85 Cats and children can often clash. Some laid-back cats w tolerate children playing nearby or petting them. If your cat has no experience with children or has a particularly nervous character, then it's likely he may avoid or react defensively toward children. If your cat has a nervous temperament, then allow him to stay away from the children altogether. Cats cannot be made to like children, b many can learn to feel happier and less fearful of them.

Action: First of all, you must take action to teach your children or visiting children to respect your cat. They should not be allowed to chase your ca lift, cuddle, or follow him about. Even the calmest cat may be traumatized by excitable children. When the time comes, you will need to show the children how to offer tidbits or gentle stroking. Supervise interactions and make sure the children understand that the cat will probably scratch or bite if they ignore your rules.

Make sure that your cat has escap routes around the house and raise beds to which he can retreat so he does not feel trapped by the children. By preventing the children from causing your cat stress, it's likely that he will begi to relax in their presence.

Left: *Children are unpredictable an often noisy, which can frighten som cats, especially when they have no opportunity to escape.*

What if my cat is scared of visitors?

86

Just because the person is your family member, a partner, or a friend, your cat doesn't know he is safe. If they visit regularly or will help to care for your cat when you go on vacation, then it's worth following a plan to teach your cat to relax.

Action: Allow your cat to watch your visitor across the room, and ask your guest not to look at the cat directly. Some cats will benefit from being placed in the security of their own basket so they can view the visitor from a distance. By spending time in the presence of a visitor who doesn't try to get close or interact, the cat learns that there's no real threat from that person. Very gradually, over many sessions, reduce the distance between visitor and cat.

When your cat can be placed near your visitor, ask the person to drop a tidbit into the basket so that a positive link is made. When your cat seems relaxed, you can open the basket and let him come out in his own time. Food can be put down to encourage him to remain in the room. Only allow the person to interact if your cat initiates it, and ensure that they remain calm and quiet while doing so. Keep interaction short to avoid overwhelming him.

Otherwise, it may be suitable to simply allow your cat the freedom to take himself out of the way during visits. You should ask all visitors to follow your rules when they come round. Never allow them to corner your cat or disturb him while he sleeps.

Above and right: There are many reasons why a visitor may be frightening for a cat with low confidence around new people. These include unfamiliar behaviors and new scents, including those coming from strange pets.

Left: Don't allow your guests to pick up or restrain your anxious cat, because he'll feel more frightened. Always allow him enough space so he can relax, and remember to praise calm behaviors.

What if my cat won't allow visitors into the house?

87

When people mention this problem it normally means that the cat is being aggressive toward the visitors, sometimes to an extreme degree. This is a huge problem, because very few people will face up to an aggressive cat. Many suffering owners no longer accept visits from friends and family due to their cat's behavioral issues.

Some cats are incredibly territorial and only allow specific family members to enter their home. They view new people as intruders and threats. Some cats are simply very fearful but have learned that aggression and threat is the best way to keep people away.

This is a serious problem that does need individual advice from a qualified behavioral specialist. Remember that cat bites and scratches can cause serious infection and injury. Until you can arrange a referral, you should keep your visitors safe by putting your cat away before you open the door.

Right: Some cats feel so threatened by visitors that they'll use great efforts to try to force them to leave. This may involve biting and scratching, especially if early signs of disturbance were left untreated.

What if my cat is lonely?

88

The first question to ask is why is your cat lonely? Has he lost a companion? Has the household changed? Are you working more often? What signs have you seen that he is lonely? Many owners who have busy lifestyles feel guilty about the lack of contact they have with their pet and then feel that they need to make up for this.

If your cat has lost a feline friend, then you may consider introducing another cat to the house. Picking a new cat to join your household does take serious consideration. You shouldn't simply choose the first kitten you see or another adult simply because it looks like the one you have lost or is a color you like. Picking the right personality to get along with your original cat is important if you are going to have a harmonious house free from stress, marking behavior and aggression. There are no guarantees, but by weighing details like your cat's temperament, age, sex, and health, you should be able to find the most suitable companion.

An adult female can be hard to introduce to a newcomer, especially if she has not had another cat around for a while. Females tend to cope better with a younger female than a rowdy, boisterous male. A male cat often gains great delight and stimulation from having another male to charge around the home and wrestle with. Try to avoid cats that are both very territorial or who have extremely different personalities, because it's easy for a timid cat to become bullied.

Far right: Some cats genuinely seem to need more social contact than others, despite the cat's ability to live a nearly solitary lifestyle. Genetics and history will influence how dependent your cat is on a companion.

Older, calm males can happily mix with young kittens and females when introduced properly. If your cat is very unsocial or unwell, think carefully about whether bringing another cat into your household is really ideal. Social problems can cause a great deal of stress both to cats and to well-meaning owners.

Always take time and care introducing cats. Getting it right from the start is always easier than trying to rectify problems later. If you do get it right, then your cat is likely to benefit greatly from having this sense of companionship, even if the relationship is not apparently the closest bond.

If another cat is out of the question, then make time each day for petting or play sessions with your cat. Regular, short sessions are better than a once-a-week splurge of attention. Try to make time for your pet or arrange for a friend or family member or even a professional pet sitter to entertain your cat during busier times.

Below: Many owners feel pressured to replace a lost cat quickly, but it's critical to choose correctly in order to ensure a smooth introduction. Don't expect the new cat to fill the shoes of the lost cat, because all relationships will differ.

Right: Arrange several play and petting sessions each day so your cat is kept entertained and doesn't feel socially deprived.

PROBLEMS OUTSIDE THE HOME

PART

4

CONTENTS

Right: *When cats venture into the great wide world outside their immediate home surroundings, they will inevitably encounter situations that can give rise to problems that an owner must address.*

INTRODUCTION

While most owner complaints and queries for advice arise when the cat is within the home or interacting with them in some way, problems also occur when the cat is outside or away from home. Often these problems involve neighbors or their animals and solving the situation can help to maintain a harmonious neighborhood. Owners often fret about leaving their cat while they go on vacation or worry about the stress involved in moving to a new house. Although cats like their familiar territory, it's possible for them to adapt to change and cope with new experiences. This section deals with some of the more common topics that may arise.

What if my cat goes into my neighbor's home?

89

A cat is naturally inclined to take advantage of any resource that seems to be available in his territory. He easily learns to follow scents of food and discover new resting places and new humans who can provide attention and petting. While these resources remain available, it's likely that your cat will continue to go into your neighbor's home.

If the neighbor dislikes his entering their home, then you need to discover how he gets in and out and why he is venturing inside. You can then agree with them to keep windows closed during the times when he is outside until he changes his ways. Alternatively, use screens on the windows to keep him out. If your neighbor has a kitty door, then it will need to be locked when not in use. By letting your neighbors know you are taking this seriously, they are less likely to resort to aversive methods without your knowledge. If necessary, you may consider using a discrete water or air spray *if* your cat still ventures into their home.

If your neighbor is encouraging your cat into his/her home, try not to feel betrayed or angry. Being upset that your cat is being unfaithful will only push him further away, and it's going to be important to have good

Left: *Cats rarely take heed of human boundaries. Open doors and windows pose great temptation, too, especially wh attention, food, or comfort are available.*

relations with your neighbor in order to overcome this problem satisfactorily. Try to explain to them that your cat does receive food and attention at home, and it's easier for you to monitor his intake and health if you are the sole provider.

However, some cats are known to frequent many different houses in a neighborhood, and in some cases different humans believe they actually "own" a cat. By having your cat microchipped, you can establish yourself as the "registered" owner. A message attached to your cat's collar may also provide unsuspecting people with information that this freeloading cat is indeed owned and well looked after.

What if my cat steals my neighbor's cat's food?

90

It can be embarrassing to discover that your cat has been raiding your neighbors' house and stealing their cat's food. Your cat has obviously discovered that a wonderful resource lies behind that door! You will need to stop him completely from gaining access, or your neighbors may discover that their own cat develops stress-related disorders due to the constant invasion. If they are using a kitty door, it may be a good idea to install a magnetic version that will only open up when their own cat approaches. The most common version requires the cat to wear a collar, but modern technology means that a special microchip version is now available where the door opens as the cat with the microchip approaches. Agree to keep your cat inside when the neighbors feed their own cat.

If your cat seems to be ravenous even though he is eating the correct amount of food provided by you before raiding the neighbors', then **seek advice from your vet**, because many medical conditions can cause problems in appetitive behavior. You will also need to think whether or not your cat is eating his own food or simply turning his nose up at your offerings and going out for dinner. Cats do like some variety in their meals, so it may help to re-think the diet you feed him.

Top of page: A raiding cat can be in and out of your property in just the blink of an eye.

Right: Intruding cats can cause extreme stress for the resident cat. A specialized kitty door that opens on signals from your cat's embedded microchip can provide the extra security needed and doesn't require a collar.

New flavors or types of food may lure cats into neighboring houses.

101

What if my cat gets bullied by our neighbor's cat?

91

Cats are naturally very territorial. Normally, they do try to avoid conflict by using scent and visual markers to signal their presence. This allows them to avoid meeting and work out a "time share" arrangement with their environment. However, sometimes aggression does occur. In a normal residential area it's very likely that the cats live much closer to one another and have to share more of the area than they would naturally.

If either cat has only recently been brought into the neighborhood, or one is maturing, then some fighting is likely. Fights often occur when the two cats are trying to move through the same area at the same time. Therefore, provide plenty of cover by strategically positioning bushy pot plants around the yard so your cat does not feel vulnerable while crossing an open area.

Walkways along fences and platforms on trees are also wonderful additions to a cat's outdoor area. For more information regarding fighting cats, see "What ifs?" nos. 62, 63, and 119.

It may help to discuss the situation with your neighbor, because neither of you wants to have to deal with cat-fight injuries. Remember that the fault does not lie with either cat in particular; the environment that they've been brought into is likely to be causing the friction in most cases. A "time share" agreement may help so the cats don't mix directly.

Above: *Cats are such popular pets they often live in territories that include several felines. When they come eye to eye, cats find themselves in situations where conflict is often unavoidable.*

Right: *Timid cats can begin to feel wary while moving through their territory and so will require plenty of opportunities to help them hide or avoid meeting others.*

What if my cat is scared of our neighbor's dog?

92 Neighborhood dogs can cause immense stress to a cat whose territory crosses those gardens. Cats are naturally a prey species, despite being such good hunters themselves. Even barking and the scent of dogs may cause great distress to some cats, and some dogs are particularly good at catching cats. The reality of how easy it is to move around the territory safely depends on the dogs involved, the cat, and the environment. Some cats continue into neighbors' yards despite scary dogs, whereas others don't venture into their own yards when they hear dogs barking next door. This again comes down to relative experience and temperament.

Ask yourself why he needs to go in the neighbor's yard. If he is going there to toilet, then it's important to make sure your cat's own area offers everything he needs. Create a private toileting area, platforms for him to sun himself on, and places where he can scratch and relax.

Above: Many dogs will react noisily, even aggressively, as they chase cats off their patch.

Above: Even a friendly, inquisitive dog can seem frightening to a cat who's unfamiliar with dogs.

What if my cat toilets in the middle of the lawn?

93 Cats that eliminate on the lawn can be both a nuisance to gardeners and a health problem to children. It can help to attract your cat to another area by creating a "latrine" with shavings or sand or a little of his favorite litter substrate. Place a little soiled material or turf on this area to signal to your cat what its purpose is. Take your cat and show him this area.

Action: Dissuade your cat from using the lawn by placing a sprinkler on the lawn (either a sensor-controlled version or one that you can turn on during his toileting times or when you spot him getting ready to toilet), scattering citrus peelings around the favored area, or sprinkling lots of pepper on the soiled spots. All these methods work to deter him from the area without reducing his confidence in you.

What if my cat digs in the flower bed?

94

Many cat owners are also gardening enthusiasts, who naturally become irritated when damaged plants are noticed; or perhaps your neighbor is getting fractious about your cat's choice of toilet area. Shooing the cat away will work temporarily, but the cat is likely to return when no one is around. It's best to change the soil substrate so that the cat decides it doesn't want to come near the area at any time. There are various options from which you can choose, depending on the size of the area. Always take care not to do something that will cause the cat harm or distress, and try to create an appropriate latrine area elsewhere; don't just assume your cat should go on someone else's property.

Action:

- Use plastic sheeting designed to deter weeds growing around your plants, and then cover it with sharp gravel or pebbles. Cocoa shell is said to work well because it's not easy for a cat to dig in. However, this can be very dangerous to dogs if ingested, so is not appropriate if you own a dog that has access to this area.
- Sprinkle generous amounts of citrus peelings or crushed pepper around the area.
- Prickly plants can be great deterrents.
- Some plants, such as the herb rue, are said to deter cats naturally. Buy some at your garden center and plant them among your bedding plants.
- Motion-triggered sprinklers are available that spray a controlled jet of water as the cat approaches. Normal sprinklers placed near the flower beds and set to come on at random times (and which can also be activated by you if you see the cat approaching) are also useful.
- Some people find metal cat silhouettes from garden centers are good deterrents, though you may not want to try this if your cat is already overly nervous. You may also need to move them around to prevent the cats from getting used to their presence and ignoring them.
- Garden centers sell lion dung which is claimed to help deter domestic cats.
- Commercial cat deterrents can be bought in powder form, though you must remember to re-administer them after heavy rain.
- An ultrasonic cat deterrent is a gadget that can help keep cats away from any area of your garden or bird feeder. It emits a burst of high-pitched sound, inaudible to human ears, when it is triggered by a cat's movement nearby.

Above: Citrus peelings are one option to deter cats.
Above: Carefully placed water sprinklers can make an area less appealing.

- Some garden centers supply scented plastic sticks that deter cats from an area of about 11 square feet (1 sq m) for up to a few weeks.
- Reflective surfaces can deter some cats, so hanging old CDs or placing semi-filled shiny plastic bottles among your bedding plants can be beneficial, although this remedy is not particularly pleasant to look at.

What if my cat eats grass?

95 Cats have no need to consume vegetation in order to meet their nutritional requirements, though the extra roughage seems to be beneficial.

Most cats are partial to eating grass from time to time. Often this is linked to a gastric complaint or possibly problems in bringing up a hairball, though little scientific evidence is available about the benefits of grass eating. It does seem to induce vomiting, which can help to release hairballs. If your cat is suddenly eating lots of grass, then consult your vet to rule out physical problems (see Part 5, "What if?" no. 139). Eating a little grass now and then is deemed normal and safe, unless the grass has been sprayed with insecticides or other chemicals. You can provide your cat with his own grass garden, which may keep him from trying to chew on your other plants. Cat grass seeds are widely available, and cocksfoot grass (*Dactylis glomerata*) is a particular favorite.

Left: *Most cats enjoy chewing shoots while out exploring. Though not an essential part of the diet, grass provides roughage.*

Above: *Grow your own trays of cat grass so that your cat has a ready supply of tempting, safe vegetation to chew on.*

What if my cat hunts birds in my yard?

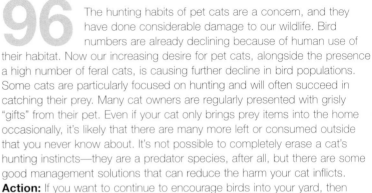

Below: Bird predation is a big concern for owners and nature enthusiasts.

The hunting habits of pet cats are a concern, and they have done considerable damage to our wildlife. Bird numbers are already declining because of human use of their habitat. Now our increasing desire for pet cats, alongside the presence a high number of feral cats, is causing further decline in bird populations. Some cats are particularly focused on hunting and will often succeed in catching their prey. Many cat owners are regularly presented with grisly "gifts" from their pet. Even if your cat only brings prey items into the home occasionally, it's likely that there are many more left or consumed outside that you never know about. It's not possible to completely erase a cat's hunting instincts—they are a predator species, after all, but there are some good management solutions that can reduce the harm your cat inflicts.

Action: If you want to continue to encourage birds into your yard, then provide them with a tall platform feeder, or use feeders that can be hung up, away from places where your cat may hide and ambush them. Many commercially available platform feeders are designed to keep cats off. Alternatively, you may wish to dissuade birds from using your yard by placing predator-shaped models or mobiles around and by removing bird feeders. This may help if your cat does not tend to roam far and if other safety options are not possible.

Help to give the birds some warning that your cat is at large so they have time to escape. Commercial collars that emit a warning sound when your cat begins to chase prey are available, though you can prepare a homemade version by **sewing several bells onto your cat's collar**. As your cat approaches, the birds will hear the jingling sound and can escape to safety. Another option is a commercially available, colorful neoprene bib that hangs down from your cat's collar while he is outside and safely reduces his ability to maneuver accurately for an attack. Cat-movement sensors are also available; they emit a high-pitched sound to keep the cat from approaching the bird feeder. However, take care with these, because some cats may be overly traumatized by the sound.

Keep your cat indoors during the times when the birds most commonl come down to feed or bathe, such as early morning or during roosting time During the winter months when birds are very hungry and likely to spend longer at bird feeders or on the ground, your cat will need to be restricted more. Keeping your cat in overnight reduces overall predation on a range of species.

Build your cat an enclosed outdoor pen where he can exercise safely at any time. This will not only help to keep wildlife safe but can also prever other problems, such as roaming and potential road traffic accidents. The enclosure can be fitted with various levels, ramps, shelters, toys, and plan so that your cat has a full and enriched time when he goes outside.

It's important that your cat have all his natural daily needs met. You cat has instincts to stalk, catch, and consume prey, and these desire can be fulfilled safely. Provide outlets for your cat's hunting instincts with exciting games indoors or in his pen. Hanging feathers, wool ball: or catnip mice can provide suitable prey for your cat to hunt, pounce o

and grab. Placing tasty treats inside boxes or hollow logs can encourage your cat to stretch and claw the pieces out. Placing your cat's food in several places around the home, rather than in the same bowl each day, will provide interest and will occupy your cat's time, leaving him with less time to develop unwanted habits.

bove: Cats are fantastic nters with large, forward- :ing eyes, sensitive aring to detect prey, d great physical agility.

ght: Even larger pets n trigger predatory havior, so supervision 'mportant for safety.

What if my cat won't get into his cat carrier?

97 This is a common problem, because often cat carriers are only brought out of the cupboard when your cat is being taken to the vets or the cattery. Your cat quickly develops a negative association with the carrier and decides that it's safer to avoid it in the future. Forcing your cat inside to make another journey to the vet will increase the problem and create further anxiety. To solve the problem, you will need to expose your cat to the carrier as much as possible while taking care not to cause him distress.

Action: Start by bringing your carrier out into a room where your cat is comfortable. Leave it open and in a place where he can investigate it in his own time. Place a familiar-smelling blanket inside the carrier and some tasty morsels to tempt your cat to investigate. Once he is comfortable entering the box, you can start to carefully close the door for short times. Drop further tasty morsels in and speak soothingly to him. Once he is comfortable doing this, move the empty carrier to a new location and allow him to familiarize himself with it again. You need to do this to prepare your cat for any situation where you may need to move him again. The pheromone spray available from your vet can help to reduce anxiety further by introducing a calming pheromone into the box. Apply two sprays shortly before putting your cat inside. ***Never force your cat into the carrier or into any other frightening situation.*** Devote time to overcoming your cat's fears now in order to significantly reduce the trauma he may feel when being taken to the vet in the future.

What if my cat is very stressed in the cattery?

98

Finding a good cattery takes time, and personal recommendations are helpful. Caring staff with plenty of tir to tend the cats in their care is vital and can help to reduc any problems your cat may have. Your cat may be feeling stressed as a re of numerous factors, including the strange smells (**left**), proximity to other cats, new people, and lack of toileting choices. The staff should be open t listening to you about your cat's personal requirements during his stay.

Bring along your cat's favorite blanket or bed, because the scer will be familiar and help to make him feel secure. A few toys may appreciated by your cat also, especially because his exercise tir may be substantially reduced compared to his normal routine. Some catteries are more relaxed and quieter than others and have more space for each cat, both inside and in the run. The will book up quickly but are worth finding and making a reservation early. It's beneficial for your cat's enclosure have a scratching post, bed area, and places to climb up, if possible. Never book your cat into a cattery th mixes unfamiliar cats or where cats can see directly into each other's pens without any privacy. If your cat particularly distressed, you may want to consider home c options instead (see "What if?" no. 99).

What if my cat has to be left while I go on vacation?

99

Cat owners have the added responsibility of making pro provision for the care of their pet while they are away fro home, whether that be overnight, for a weekend, or for a long vacation. Cats should never be left to fend for themselves, despite th perceived independence. There are different options for the care of your c while you are away:

- **Home Care:** Some cats cope better if they can remain in their own ho while their owner is away. Family or friends may be willing to take on ca duties each day. They will need to provide food and water, clean litter trays, and spend some time providing your cat with games or company. You will need to leave clear instructions about the amo of food (leave enough), medications (what/when/how to give), and your vet's telephone number and address in case of emergencies. It's a good idea to change your cat's ID tag tempor to the caregiver's number so he/she can be contacted in case o emergency. Remember to leave your cat carrier out, too.
- **Professional Home Boarder:** If no personal friends are available, professional pet sitting services may suit your needs. Ask your vet to recommend a service, and check their credentials a insurance. They should have proof of a background check by police t give you peace of mind, because they will have access to your home.

Above: Plan ahead so that your cat is comfortable while you're away.

- **Cat Hotel:** Using a cattery is an option for cats who dislike new peopl their home or when you don't want a virtual stranger in your home. Aga ask your vet and friends to recommend a cattery. Go and visit it, meet

staff, and see where your cat will be kept. You will be able to judge its suitability for your cat and can discuss your cat's requirements with them. Most catteries will require evidence of current vaccinations before they accept your cat into their care, which is as much for your own cat's protection as for the protection of others. Most catteries will allow you to bring in an item with familiar scents to help reassure your cat.

What if my cat gets lost?

100

Although cats can be very elusive, most pets have routines that are known by their owners. When a cat disappears there are certain things that should be done to maximize the probability of his return. Stay positive, because most missing cats will return home, and there are many stories of cats coming home after long periods away.

Male cats tend to roam further from home than others, especially if the animal has not been neutered. In this case you will need to check your whole area. Call your local rescue shelters, catteries, and vets to make sure they are on the lookout. Also advertise around your area so people can report any sightings to you and know to check their sheds, garages, and greenhouses.

Housecats will be very frightened if they have accidentally found themselves outdoors and been unable to get back in. It's likely that this cat will be hiding somewhere very close to home but too afraid to come out, even to your voice. Self-protection is your cat's main priority in this scenario, and he will probably remain in hiding until the environment quiets down.

Ensuring that your cat is microchipped will mean that if found, whether as a stray or through an accident, he can be scanned and identified. Collars and tags bearing your contact details are also useful, although they may be lost and so are not a foolproof method of identification.

Note: If you are using a collar, please make sure that it's **not too tight or too loose**, because both can be catastrophic. A tight collar may cause skin/tissue damage or breathing difficulties, while a collar that's too loose may allow your cat to get his leg or even his jaw caught in it, or it may get snagged on something. Elastic cat collars can provide just enough give to release a trapped cat without being too restrictive.

Above and right: Microchipping your cat is a useful procedure so that he carries your contact information with him, allowing easy identification and a safe return.

109

What if my cat roams far from home?

101

A cat's territory size can vary immensely between individuals. Where the area is densely populated with cats, an individual may occupy a territory that is split into several different areas. Your cat may have to travel to reach each part of his territory, which may provide him with different resources. Male cats typically roam further, and intact (unneutered) males have been known to travel several miles to visit a female in heat. Castration will reduce his desire to seek females and curb much of the roaming instincts. Make sure he has all he needs within your home grounds, including attention, entertainment, feeding and watering areas, and safe resting and toileting spots.

What if my cat brings prey into the house?

102

The action of bringing in gifts for owners will occur from time to time in most cats. It's more common in female cats, but males also do it. Queens naturally hunt and bring prey into the kittens to teach them how to hunt and kill. Although this can be unsavory, it's unfair to punish a cat for bringing you these presents, because you are likely to simply cause anxiety—after all, cats don't realize that owners find it distasteful to wake up to a mouse or a frog in their slipper!

If the "gift" happens to still be alive, then you will need to calmly recapture and free it or safely dispose of the remains should it then expire. Capturing live prey is best done by trapping it under an upside-down container to allow you to restrict its movement without risking being bitten or harming the animal.

Left: Try to satisfy your cat's hunting desires by providing stimulating games and "pretend" prey that he can catch inside the home.

What if my cat won't hunt mice?

103

The hunting instinct varies between individual cats. Your cat's desire to hunt and catch mice is influenced by his early experiences as a kitten, his breed (which will influence his ability to hunt), and his health. You cannot force your cat to hunt mice, so you would be better off investing in mousetraps placed in safe places where your cat is unlikely to trigger them or in another cat with a known hunting ability (see "What if?" no. 79). Remember that your new "mouser" may also hunt other small animals around your property too.

What if my cat has to move to a new house with us?

104

Moving to a new house is known to be a stressful time for humans, and our cats agree. However, there are many things that you can do to make sure that your move goes smoothly and your cat settles into his new home as quickly as possible.

Action: Agree on the routine with your family before your moving day so that everyone understands what has been planned. Restrict your cat to one room on the day you move. He should have a litter box, food, and water. Lock the door if possible, or place a clear sign on the door to remind people not to open it. Make sure your movers or friends also understand that this room is out of bounds. Once all the furniture and boxes have been removed and the house is empty, you can then put your cat in his carrier and pack up his remaining things, which can travel with you so that you have them available as soon as you arrive. Your cat should wear a collar and tag with your up-to-date contact details.

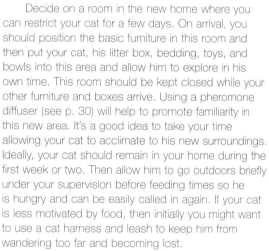

Below: Moving involves huge changes to your cat's environment well before moving day. Cats are often lost during this period, so take care to prevent your cat from climbing into a packing box or the moving van or from escaping outside.

Decide on a room in the new home where you can restrict your cat for a few days. On arrival, you should position the basic furniture in this room and then put your cat, his litter box, bedding, toys, and bowls into this area and allow him to explore in his own time. This room should be kept closed while your other furniture and boxes arrive. Using a pheromone diffuser (see p. 30) will help to promote familiarity in this new area. It's a good idea to take your time allowing your cat to acclimate to his new surroundings. Ideally, your cat should remain in your home during the first week or two. Then allow him to go outdoors briefly under your supervision before feeding times so he is hungry and can be easily called in again. If your cat is less motivated by food, then initially you might want to use a cat harness and leash to keep him from wandering too far and becoming lost.

If you are only moving a short distance from your old home, then your cat may find his way back "home." Let the new owners know how to contact you if they find he has returned. In this case, you may need to let more time elapse before he's allowed to roam freely. The longer he spends within his new environment, the stronger his attachment to it will be.

What if my cat hates traveling by car?

105

Most cats dislike traveling away from home. They are normally not used to doing so and only travel now and again to go to the vet. A familiar home territory is vital for a cat's feeling of relaxation, and the sudden change and novelty of traveling makes it very likely that your cat will feel stressed.

Action: To minimize any feelings of insecurity associated with traveling, follow these tips.

- Introduce your cat to his secure carrier early so he feels very comfortable (see "What if?" no. 97). Never allow him to move about freely when traveling in your vehicle.
- Be careful when moving the carrier so your cat is not jolted about. This includes making sure it's securely positioned in your car and that you brake and make turns as smoothly as possible.
- Spray a pheromone diffuser (see p. 30) into your car about 20 minutes before your journey, as directed.
- Don't feed your cat a heavy meal prior to traveling, because he may be sick.
- Try short practice journeys over a number of weeks before your planned trip to help desensitize your cat to being in the car.
- Plan your stops to ensure your cat has plenty of water.
- Your vet may prescribe medication for motion sickness for severely distressed cats.
- If overnight stops are needed, book a pet-friendly hotel in advance. Remember to bring your cat's litter box.
- Your cat should be wearing a collar with a tag during your journey, just in case he escapes. The tag should provide a mobile phone number or a contact number that you will have access to while away from home.
- Never leave your cat locked inside your car, because he may overheat.

Below: Always use a familiar and safe cat carrier to transport your cat; avoid open cardboard boxes, and don't let him travel loose as he could escape.

Right: Secure transport is critical, because a frightened cat could escape in a parking lot or roadside stop and put himself in danger. Always ensure he travels wearing current ID tags.

What if my cat likes sunbathing?

106

Cats are known to be avid sun-worshippers and can normally be found following sunbeams around. Despite loving the warmth, it's important to encourage your cat to spend some time in the shade to avoid overheating. White or pale-colored cats can burn easily, and cancers can develop on the thin-skinned ear and nose areas from overexposure to the sun. If your cat is prone to sun damage, then you should apply sunscreen suitable for cats. Never apply your own sunscreen without first checking with your vet, because it may be toxic to cats and cause further problems when he grooms himself. If you do see lesions or unusual marks on your cat's skin, **please seek advice from your vet**, because feline skin cancers can be treated well if caught early. Also ensure that your cat can have access fresh water at all times.

Be careful if your cat likes to seek out warmth in your open greenhouse or those of your neighbors. Make sure that you remember to check for any feline presence inside the greenhouse before you close the door—and ask your neighbors to check when they do so too. The intense heat inside is extremely dangerous to cats who may get trapped there.

Above and below: Cats are well known as lovers of warmth and can often be found stretched out in the sunniest areas.

What if my cat is going to experience our party?

107

Before any type of party, it's best to arrange for your cat to be in a safe place so you can relax and enjoy yourself. Some cats cope well, but others find the noise and intrusion distressing. If your cat copes well when staying in the cattery, then this is a valid and fairer option for the night when you are holding a big party. If the party is not going to last long and you have a secure area in which to keep your cat, then this is also a possibility. If you are planning on having fireworks, remember that the loud sounds and explosions could cause him distress. Don't allow him outdoors as the time of the fireworks event approaches. This is a good rule on all evenings when fireworks are likely and during events like Halloween and New Year's Eve.

Action: Make the room where he is being kept as secure as possible by closing all windows and doors, drawing the curtains, and turning on the TV or music to help cover up some of the noises from the party. A sign on the door will remind family and guests not to enter. Set up a litter box in the room and allow him to investigate his new surroundings before the evening's events begin. Make sure that your cat's ID tag and microchip information are up-to-date in case he does manage to escape. Your cat may feel happier being

Above: Cats, like other pets, can be terrified of loud noises; many people create a safe area at home or book a cattery.

Right: Your cat can enjoy some features of the party when it is all over!

left in his carrier, because cats do like smaller, secure spaces. If your cat becomes highly distressed during fireworks or other noisy events which are likely to occur, then either arrange for alternative housing arrangements for those nights or discuss the situation with your vet, who may be able to suggest suitable medication to help to keep him relaxed.

What if my cat won't go outside?

108

If your cat has never experienced the world outdoors, then he may be reluctant to venture outside. Other cats may refuse to go out because of problems they may already have encountered, such as another cat. Many cats simply won't go outside if the weather is bad. Each cat will need his own personal suggestions, because each cat has his own reasons for remaining indoors.

It's never a good idea to force a cat to go outdoors before he is ready. This may make his fears worse or cause him to start avoiding you. Try to **address his fears** (refer to the "What if?" question that most closely deals with your cat's particular problem), and then gradually begin to encourage him outdoors by using tidbits and games. Take your time, because he may need to build up his confidence again. Be prepared to provide more cover as part of your outdoor area, and enrich your home environment so that your cat is happy and satisfied at all times. A safe outdoor enclosure may be an option, because your cat won't have to encounter other cats, traffic, or people that might have caused him to be fearful in the first place. If your adult cat has previously always been an indoor cat, then you may have to accept that this is the lifestyle he knows and that his socialization experiences have not provided him with the ability to cope with the outdoor world. Spend your time creating an interesting indoor environment for him instead.

ove: Your cat may feel *'est* indoors, especially *is* early socialization *'* not involve outdoor *eriences.* Some cats *n* gradually learn to *apt* during short, *asant* excursions into *outside* world.

ght: Some cats will *gin* to avoid the *doors* after a particularly *ntening* experience. Try *discover* what that was, *1* make changes to your *door* area to boost your *'s* confidence.

PREVENTING AND COPING WITH ILLNESS

Francesca Riccomini BSc(Hons), BVetMed, MRCVS, DAS(CABC), CCAB, Dip Arch

PART 5

CONTENTS

- **INTRODUCTION** Page 118

What if my cat . . .

INTRODUCTION

Cat owners are understandably fascinated by their pet's behavior, b when it comes to the recognizing the difference between health and disease, it's important to the veterinarian as well, because many medical problems present no evidence other than a change in behavior. However, in the wild a potential meal never wants to draw attention to the fact he's under par and vulnerable. So, as cats are not only predators but a prey species too, changes that alert us to a potential problem are often subtle and need skilful interpretation.

In the clinic, behavior also helps in establishing what's wrong, because the nature of changes generally indicates what body systems may be affected and the likely underlying cause. This determines the investigations required to aid diagnosis and indicates appropriate treatment, while behavio again indicates if we're on the right track and that treatment is helping to return the pet to health. Obviously the earlier that signs of trouble are spotte and the veterinarian consulted the better. So never allow lack of time or lac of confidence in your judgement to get in the way of quickly seeking help, because once conditions are well established, they're often more complicated.

Above: Getting to know your cat's normal behavior patterns will help you to spot signs that indicate that all is not well.

Of course, it's not only when things go wrong that owners and vets work together to benefit the cats that share our lives. Preventive health care is a major part of veterinary practice and responsible ownership. Additionall regular routine presentations at the clinic provide the opportunity for forging relationships with an individual veterinarian, who the has the advantage, when things go wrong, of knowing how particular patient looked, acted, and felt when he was well.

Below: Enlightened, caring vets and owners work together to reduce the stress of feline veterinary visits.

Choosing a Veterinary Practice

When choosing a veterinary practice, it's advisable to avoid simply letting convenience dictate where we register. Cats a now the most popular pet in several countries, and are getting the consideration they deserve in medical terms. In the Unite States, The Humane Society has helped to raise awareness of the special needs of feline patients, particularly in relation to handling and provision of suitable facilities. Even so, in the veterinary world different attitudes and aptitudes prevail, so it pays to seek empathetic, skilled practitioners who deal sensitively with both pets and owners. Otherwise th cumulative effect of stressful veterinary visits can res in cats becoming difficult to handle, examine, and tre with owners dreading the consultation with the vet tha needed to ensure their companion receives the professional attention necessary to maintain good health. The best approach is to find a practice that suits you and your pet before you need it by:

- asking other cat owners for recommendations.
- chatting to staff.
- finding out about after-hours emergency coverage.
- requesting to look round the facilities at a convenient time.

It's also useful to bring any specific problems that affect your pet or any special needs that either of you may have to the receptionist's attention. A practice will be better placed to deal with the situation if staff members are already alerted, for example, to the fact that you could need help carrying your cat basket or that your pet has a complicated and long-standing medical history or has recently been "rescued" and needs particularly sensitive handling.

Owners can also contribute to the smooth running of veterinary visits by having all a pet's relevant documents together in a file that's handy, particularly in a crisis. Keeping vaccination records up to date and noting major or minor accidents, illnesses, surgical interventions, drug reactions, or special diets will enable a clinician during routine or emergency presentations of your cat to quickly review pertinent issues that may affect the clinical approach on this occasion.

What if my cat is ill and I don't notice?

109

Cats are not noisy, exuberant, and social animals like dogs. They generally choose to hide away as a strategy for avoiding trouble when they don't feel 100 percent. So cat owners are right to be concerned about missing warning signs, especially because felines sleep for much of their time, and spotting lethargy can sometimes be problematic! However, many illnesses are associated with certain clinical signs, and although these may be subtle in nature, close observation is likely to pick them up, even if a pet is not by instinct a "lap" cat and spends little time at home. It's often changes in **behavioral patterns** that draw attention to an injury or medical condition, so any owner who's familiar with what his or her cat does is unlikely to be negligent. Anyway, it's far better to make an unnecessary trip to the veterinarian than risk overlooking something that's amiss.

Above: Making notes beforehand will help your vet to help your pet!

Right: Hiding is a normal feline coping strategy, but excessive withdrawal could indicate your cat needs veterinary attention.

What if my cat lives entirely indoors?

110

If their cats don't go outside, and they're diligent, observant owners, some people wonder if there's any need to present them when clinic check-up and vaccination reminders arrive. The answer is "Yes," so that clinicians get to know you, and because some conditions may give little outward sign until a crisis is precipitated. It's an especially unlucky individual for whom indications that such conditions may develop aren't highlighted by regular routine attendance, particularly for vulnerable age groups, the most junior and senior pets, or breeds with known predispositions to specific problems, for instance. Then owners will be told what to look out for, and preventive or supportive treatment will be instigated.

Routine visits also flag minor issues that are sometimes overlooked by those most closely involved with a pet. For example, a slow, insidious piling on of the pounds or the opposite—a gradual weight loss. Or small but significant expansion of skin lumps that become more difficult to deal with if left too long, because everyone at home has simply adjusted to their increasing size!

What if my cat is ill— what signs will I see?

111

It's changes that count. Hence the importance of getting used to any individual cat's "normal" condition! **Appetite:** Increase (polyphagia), decrease, or loss (anorexia) can all be significant, especially if the effect on weight is the opposite of what would be expected.

Clearly, discretion needs to be exercised before panic sets in. If, for example, the reduced appetite is a recent occurrence and coincides with a new type of diet, a different brand of food, or alteration in its recipe that's no so palatable, there's probably no need to worry. But if a loss of interest and appetite are seen for no apparent reason or coincide with other changes in appearance and/or behaviour, it merits a checkup.

Weight: Excess weight (*left*) is unhealthy and predisposes companion animals to a range of potential problems. Because changing human lifestyle in many societies have resulted in different expectations of pets, the increased prevalence of indoor cats and of treating pets as "part of the family," for example, obesity is more common and problematic than previously. The solution to this issue is a combined medical and behavioral approach.

On the other hand, weight loss, especially when combined with increased appetite or thirst, indicates a range of potential problems. So unless your pet is on a dedicated weight reduction program, it should quickly lead to a veterinarian visit.

Thirst: Increased thirst (polydypsia) is often most significant, with a range of pathological problems potentially underlying it. It's important to

Above: *Having fun with water is fine—but excessive thirst or a change of drinking pattern often indicates ill health.*

assess the actual amount of fluid your cat consumes, although often it's a change of drinking pattern that alerts us to problems. For example, many cats, particularly those on wet food, are rarely seen drinking. Therefore, if they're spotted lapping from puddles, birdbaths, watering cans, or glasses of water, it's wise to bring this to the veterinarian's attention. It may simply reflect high indoor temperatures during winter or a heat wave that's making numerous pets thirsty, but it's better to be safe than sorry.

Lethargy: Energy naturally waxes and wanes during the 24-hour cycle. Cats are generally more active at dawn and dusk; they rest more as a result of vigorous activity or high ambient temperature. However, if a pet that's normally out and about much of the day and actively interacts with owners when home suddenly sits around and/or sleeps instead, things could be going wrong. He needs veterinary attention, especially if decreased activity and increased lethargy coincide with any other changes, or your cat's generally bright, sparkling eyes appear dull and his animated expression is replaced by a pinched look.

Stiffness/lameness: Cats are renowned for their fluid movement and graceful elegance. Any loss of weight-bearing ability, lameness, swelling of the limbs or joints, or even just stiffness on rising or reluctance to jump is potentially significant, whether it's extreme and sudden in onset or relatively innocuous, becoming more gradually apparent. Clearly, traumatic injury leading to wounds, breaks (fractures), dislocations, or strains and sprains of ligaments and muscles is a feature of feline medicine and surgery; sadly, tumors can develop in any part of the orthopedic system (the bones and muscles), resulting in pain, disability, swelling, even pathological fractures. The latter are, however, rare when compared with everyday accidents and "wear and tear" conditions. Tumors all too frequently go unrecognized and untreated. This is of concern now that we're able, through a combination of better husbandry, nutrition, and veterinary care, to keep cats well into their teens, when like us they're more prone to aging conditions, such as arthritis. The continuous discomfort from such chronic conditions can erode an animal's well-being and quality of life if no one realizes what's happening and initiates a suitable treatment program. This is another good reason for attending regular senior pet clinics. ▶

Above: *Never ignore unusual tiredness. Lethargy can be a cat's first sign of illness.*

Right: *Veterinarians use a variety of investigative techniques in addition to physical examination and the information owners provide to diagnose illness.*

Above: Regularly check your cat's fur. Act quickly if you notice anything unusual.

Appearance: Sleek and glossy coats are a feline characteristic, so changes may suggest the onset of a problem. Loss of condition resulting from simple lack of normal grooming behavior that keeps fur in good shape, hair loss, or matting of the coat, so that hair clumps and sticks up in spikes, have many causes. They range from simple reduction in energy levels, through mouth pain, to significant illness involving major organs, such as liver and kidneys, all of which require prompt medical intervention.

Equally, if you notice excessive grooming, check for signs of problems and ensure you're up to date with routine external parasite control. Do consult your vet if you find a wound, any signs of hair loss, or if your cat's skin looks red, sore, scabby or scaly (scurf/dandruff).

In addition, don't delay taking your pet to the clinic if you observe:

- Vomiting
- Diarrhea
- Blood loss
- Discharges
- Coughing
- Sneezing
- Breathing problems
- Difficulty eliminating
- Wobbliness
- Loss of balance or collapse

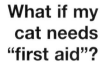

Pain: Feline behavior has developed so that cats give little away to competitors and potential predators in the wild. As a result, when they're in pain, cats rarely howl, cry out, or hiss unless touched where it hurts. They generally express pain and distress by "turning in on themselves," or sometimes purring loudly, possibly as a means of reassuring themselves or soliciting care from owners. Of course, this doesn't mean that when your cat is behaving normally, he's hiding a painful condition from you. But if his usual behavior patterns or appearance change, if he's abnormally silent or excessively vocal, do seek your veterinarian's advice at the earliest opportunity. The sooner problems are detected, the better the outcome is likely to be.

What if my cat needs "first aid"?

112

There are a number of occasions when cats get int trouble and owners need to think clearly and act fast. It's wise to plan ahead so you'll know what to do if your pet has an accident or is suddenly taken ill. Also make sure that the essential equipment and the important telephone numbers you might need, such as your veterinary clinic and their emergency service, are read available. Do include your cat's carrier box, a towel or blanket suitable for use as a stretcher/sling, and a small hot water bottle plus something to wrap it in so you can keep your pet warm without the risk of burns while in transit to the veterinary clinic.

Your first aid kit:
Antiseptic ointment/cream/solution—ask your vet's advice.
- Table salt—to make a dilute saline solution for bathing minor skin wounds. Do this by adding about half a teaspoonful of salt to a large glass of warm water.
- Sterile dressing pads.
- Absorbant cotton—a wide roll as well as smaller swabs so you can make up pressure pads to staunch bleeding if necessary.
- Bandages—two or three different widths.
- Self-adhesive bandage.
- Roll of narrow adhesive tape.
- Scissors and tweezers—blunt not pointed.
- Latex gloves.
- Potential tourniquet, say a flat tape or cord.
- Cold pack—keep one (or a small bag of peas) in the freezer. If you need to use it—for example, for a nose bleed or to reduce swelling from stings or injuries—always wrap it well to avoid excessive chilling of tissues.

Below: A promptly applied dressing will help prevent contamination and stop your cat from licking his wound, which may cause more damage. However, it's important to make sure that the bandage is not too tight.

What you should do
- Keep calm.
- Think carefully.
- Don't act rashly.
- When you do approach your pet, be careful. If he's hurt, frightened, distressed, or in pain, any cat may act uncharacteristically and inadvertently injure you with teeth or claws.
- If your pet is in a hazardous position, gently move him to a safe place. If he's collapsed or disabled by injury, for example, roll or lift him onto a blanket or towel, taking care to support all his weight and not unnecessarily displace his limbs or compress his body as you do so.
- Ensure his airway is clear by cautiously removing any discharges from his mouth and gently pulling his tongue out of his mouth if necessary. At the same time, check the color of his gums, which are likely to be pale if he's in shock or suffering from blood loss or a bluish color if his respiration is compromised. In the latter case, ensure there's no obstruction at the back of his throat
- Artificial respiration or cardiac massage require experience, so seek immediate veterinary help unless you are trained in these procedures.
- Administer crucial first aid if you understand what is needed. If you're not sure what to do, telephone your veterinarian's office with paper and pen to hand to write down numbers, addresses, and instructions. Concisely describe the situation and ask for advice in handling your pet and dealing with his specific condition.

What if my cat is bleeding?

113

Internal bleeding results in cold extremities and pale gums. Sometimes blood also oozes from a pet's nostrils, mouth, or anus, so clear any nasal discharge to make sure your cat can breathe and doesn't choke. There's little else you can do except handle him calmly and gently, keep him warm and quiet, and *get veterinary assistance as quickly as possible.*

If he is bleeding from an external wound, locate it, then if it's small, bathe it clean with an antiseptic solution, say dilute saline, before applying a sterile dressing. It's wise, though, to get cuts checked, because infection can set in. *It's crucial to seek medical attention quickly if bleeding is severe.* Meanwhile, apply an appropriately sized bandage to the area if you can, winding it tight enough to exert pressure but not so much that the blood supply will be cut off.

If a badly bleeding limb needs a tourniquet, apply a flat tape to an area between the bleed and the heart, and then twist it to stem the blood flow, but time when you started to make sure you *don't keep it tight for more than 15 minutes*. This is a strictly short-term maneuver while on your way to obtain professional help.

Above: A tourniquet is an emergency option to help stem bleeding.

What if my cat is in shock?

114

As with internal bleeding, if cats suffer from shock, their paws and ears tend to be cold to the touch, the gums are pale, breathing is shallow, and the body is floppy. The best action is to check that his airway is clear, keep your pet quiet and warm, say by laying him on a well-wrapped hot water bottle and placing a light blanket over him, and contact your clinic's emergency service for instruction.

What if my cat is electrocuted?

115

Never touch your cat until he has been isolated from the electricity source. Switch off the current or use a wooden broom handle to push him away from it. *Immediately seek your vet's help* while keeping your pet warm and quiet.

What if my cat is burned or scalded?

116

Prompt action is required to reduce tissue damage from heat or corrosive chemical contamination. Cool the affected area with cold water, ice packs, or wet towels. Don't apply ointment or dressings, but make sure your cat doesn't lick himself, say by wrapping him in a towel while you're in transit to the veterinary clinic.

What if my cat is involved in an accident?

117

- Remove your pet carefully to a safe place. See page 123, "What if?" no. 112 for advice on how to do this.
- Assess the situation.
- Ensure he can breathe and his airway is clear.
- Deal with any bleeding.
- Confining him to his carrier should help avoid further damage if he has a fracture, dislocation, or internal injuries.
- Keeping him warm and placing him in a quiet dark room will help with shock and stress.
- ***Telephone your veterinarian's clinic for medical advice and get him there as soon as possible*** for your vet to assess his condition.

What if my cat is poisoned?

118

Cats aren't naturally well equipped to cope with ingested toxic substances, so they're susceptible to poisoning by a range of products used in the home and yard—for instance anti-freeze, disinfectants, pesticides, and common drugs like acetaminophen. If your pet may have eaten, licked, or drunk something potentially harmful, ***do not try to make him vomit.*** Call for emergency advice with details of the products involved so veterinary staff can help. If the noxious substance has contaminated your cat's fur, make sure he can't clean himself; confine him to his carrier so you can observe him for signs such as dribbling, vomiting, or staggering, and get help quickly.

You may be advised to clean his coat with warm water and liquid detergent, ***although it's best to get directions that are relevant to your actual circumstances in case such action is not appropriate and can make things worse.***

What if my cat is caught in a cat fight?

119

Although often ferocious, fights between cats may not do any obvious damage. However, this can be misleading because their mouths contain bacteria, so even a small wound can become infected. Consequently, post-battle punctures that appear as nothing more than a scab with a matted tuft of hair should never be neglected. Clip the hair using blunt-tipped scissors, then bathe the affected area twice a day with warm dilute saline solution. But don't delay a veterinary trip if the surrounding skin is sore or the wound is large, deep, or discharging. Antibiotics are often necessary to prevent abscess formation.

bove: When advised to athe your cat, ask your terinarian what shampoo/ etergent to use.

ght: Check your cat refully after a fight. ncture wounds aren't vays obvious initially.

What if my cat is caught in a house fire?

120

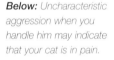

- Remove your cat from the danger area.
- Place him somewhere quiet, dark, and well ventilated to calm down.
- Deal with any of the issues needing first aid.
- Prevent him from licking himself, as his fur may be contaminated.
- Seek professional help.

Even if your pet has not been injured, pneumonia can develop from smoke inhalation and is a serious risk. We're better at preventing this than in the past, but treatment needs to be immediate and sometimes aggressive with steam inhalations, physiotherapy, and oxygen therapy used to help affected cats clear smoke debris from their lungs. **So act with speed,** acquaint your vet with as much detail about what happened to your pet as possible, and ask searching questions about what treatment he will receive.

Below: Uncharacteristic aggression when you handle him may indicate that your cat is in pain.

What if my cat hisses and spits when I pick him up?

121

If your pet is normally amenable to handling, such behavior can indicate fear and/or pain. Put him down immediately, or you risk getting hurt, increasing his distress, and possibly making things worse if he's injured. Don't let him escape; gently examine him (from a distance if necessary), looking for any unusual physical signs, breathing difficulty, or a limp, for instance. Take note of the circumstances: is something stressful happening in the environment or social group, or has he just rushed in from outside, suggesting he's been involved in a fight or accident? Darken the room and keep him quiet while you decide on your course of action, which should obviously include a veterinary visit unless you can put your finger on something minor and straightforward. (See also Part 3, "What if?" no. 66)

What if my cat needs preventive care—what does this mean?

122

We're able to protect cats against a number of infectious diseases, internal and external parasites, and dental disease. Measures aimed at preventing problems come under the umbrella of preventive care.

The list should also include identification of pets, because your vet can easily implant a small microchip under your cat's skin. Each has a unique number registered with your contact details on a central computer, so if your pet wanders or is involved in an accident, you'll be able to locate him. It's useful to have some additional visible means of identification, such as a collar with your details inscribed on a tag; then anyone needing to contact you can easily do so. However, make sure your pet's collar will snap if he gets it caught, but don't be tempted to leave it very loose. It could get snagged over his lower jaw or behind his front leg. Troublesome injuries can arise from collars digging into the skin and the underlying tissues.

What if my cat isn't vaccinated?

123

(See also "What ifs?" nos. 111 and 128.) Neglecting this important area of preventive care leaves your cat vulnerable to diseases for which we have reliable vaccines. These include:

Feline panleukopenia (feline infectious enteritis [FIE] or feline parvovirus)

This viral disease causes severe vomiting and diarrhea, which can be fatal within a few hours, especially in kittens and young cats. It is spread via infected feces and is less common than it was because of the efficacy of the vaccine. (See also "What ifs?" nos. 140 and 150.)

Feline herpesvirus (cat flu)
Feline calicivirus (cat flu)

Cat flu causes high temperature, sneezing, nasal discharge, runny eyes, and sometimes painful ulceration of the tongue and damage to the cornea of the eye. Depending upon the strain contracted, infected cats may be affected for life and intermittently shed virus if they're stressed. While cat flu is not generally a killer, because of the particular susceptibility of young and elderly cats and the long-term risks it should always be taken seriously. (See also "What ifs?" nos. 130, 131, 132, and 135.)

Feline leukemia virus (FeLV)

Spread in infected saliva, this virus attacks the immune system, so signs vary and may not show until some time after infection. They include weight loss, lack of appetite and lethargy, and relate to cancer, which ranges from leukemia affecting the blood cells to tumors of the lymphatic system in a number of common sites, especially the chest and abdomen. (See also "What ifs?" nos. 140, 141, 145, 146, and 147.)

Chlamydophila felis

This bacterium causes conjunctivitis (inflammation and swelling of the eyelids) and signs of upper respiratory infection, that is, runny eyes and nose, sneezing, and coughing. It is spread by direct contact between cats and is usually treated with antibiotics, but a vaccine is available. (See also "What if?" no. 132.)

Bordetella bronchiseptica

Another bacterial infection, this is one of the infectious agents that cause "kennel cough" in dogs. Vaccination is via a nose drop vaccine, which, although not routine, is considered in some circumstances, for instance if cats go into a boarding cattery, live in a susceptible multi-cat household, or share their homes with dogs. (See also "What ifs?" nos. 132 and 135.) ▶

Above: *Never delay if you notice signs of discharge or blood around your cat's nose. He may have had an accident or be ill. The sooner he receives veterinary attention, the better his chances will be.*

Right: *Effective vaccines have greatly reduced the incidence of several infectious diseases. Remember that regular boosters are essential to maintain immunity. Your veterinarian will recommend the ideal regimen for your cat.*

Below: Unvaccinated kittens are especially susceptible to preventable diseases. Prompt vaccination is essential to provide them with maximum protection.

Rabies

This deadly disease affects the nervous system, causing changes in behavior: initially brief subtle depression, followed by furious aggression, then paralysis. **There is no cure for rabies and it is transmissible to humans.** Absent in some countries, it is unfortunately a real threat in many areas of the world. A vaccine is available, and information about the local situation should always be obtained from embassy staff or your own officials if you are planning to travel to other countries with your cat.

Where the disease does not exist, permission from the relevant government department is generally necessary before a pet can be vaccinated. If you live in an area where rabies is endemic, your veterinary clinic staff will advise you about the local situation and vaccine policy.

Don't forget . . . always discuss the appropriate vaccination regimen for your cat with your veterinarian, who will be aware of conditions in your area, the relevance of your pet's medical history, and his lifestyle. For example, it is often recommended not to routinely vaccinate indoor-only cats against FeLV, but in your particular circumstances there may be a good reason why you should do so. Additionally, some vaccines are available in some countries but not licensed for use in others.

Below: Close observation helps vets diagnose or rule out a range of conditions.

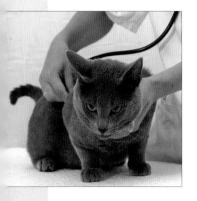

Do these vaccines cover all the infectious feline diseases?

Sadly, there are other potentially fatal feline diseases for which no vaccine is as yet universally available. Principally these are:

Feline immunodeficiency virus (FIV)

This viral infection is similar to HIV, though it is not transmissible from cats to people. The effects relate to immune compromise and are similar in both species. Affected individuals can remain well for some time or succumb quite quickly, showing a variety of signs including weight loss, lethargy, loss of appetite, vomiting, diarrhea, gum infections, and eye and skin disorders. FIV is spread mainly through cat bites, vulnerable cats sharing food bowls with infected individuals, or mothers passing it to their offspring. There is no cure, but fortunately blood tests can identify cats that have developed a carrier status, so they can be isolated to prevent further spread. (See also "What ifs?" nos. 129, 140, 142, and 146.)

Feline infectious peritonitis (FIP)

This is caused by a coronavirus, spread via feces and saliva, which, despite being very infectious, only causes problems in some cats. Immuno compromised and/or stressed cats are most susceptible, so FIP is particularly problematic in multi-cat groups. It can affect any of the body's systems and has similar symptoms to many diseases, making it often diffic to diagnose. In some affected cats fluid accumulates in the body cavities. Others are lethargic, have vomiting and diarrhea, or show neurological sig.

as the brain and nervous system are affected, resulting in strange behavior or even blindness. Unfortunately, because there is no cure, once cats develop actual signs of the disease, treatment focuses on using any supportive medication, such as appetite stimulants and anti-inflammatory drugs, that may be effective, given the nature of the individual cat's clinical signs. (See also "What ifs?" nos. 135, 146, and 147.)

Feline infectious anemia (FIA)

FIA is caused by *Haemobartonella felis*. Two species of this bacterium can parasitize red blood cells, causing depression, weight loss, breathing difficulties, and sometimes collapse. We've much to learn about this disease, but because it's more common in older males, fighting is considered a means of transmission; bites from fleas are a suspected method, and it does appear to be transferred from mothers to their very young offspring.

Symptoms can wax and wane, with cats being most susceptible to serious illness if they're stressed or suffering immune compromise as a result of other diseases, such as FIV or FeLV. Consequently, it's important to pay attention to regular flea control and deal with any aggression problems within feline groups.

Treatment is with antibiotics and corticosteroids, although severe anemia requires blood transfusions. (See also "What if?" no. 135.)

Toxoplasmosis

Toxoplasma gondii causes this parasitic disease that affects many warm-blooded species, including felines. But while a high percentage of cats are infected, illness is uncommon because many become immune. Symptoms vary from lack of appetite, lethargy, diarrhea, and weight loss to respiratory distress due to complications affecting major organs.

Treatment is by a combination of antibiotics and other drugs, and young cats are especially susceptible.

Although there is never room for complacency, the main concern generally is that **this is a zoonosis**, a disease transmissible from animals to people, with pregnant women and their unborn babies being especially at risk. However, this is a very common parasite worldwide, with human infections often linked to eating contaminated vegetables and undercooked meat. Consequently, good hygiene, particularly with food preparation, is crucial, and sensible precautions should always be taken when emptying cat litter boxes and gardening in areas used as cat latrines. Women in the high-risk category should avoid such activities, others should wear disposable rubber gloves, and children's sand boxes should be covered when they're not in use. (See also "What if?" no. 142.)

bove: If you have trouble edicating your cat, scuss the best method ith your vet and ask for a emonstration of how it ould be done.

ght: Combining the formation you provide out your pet's mptoms with her own servations will help your terinarian make a ovisional diagnosis. ing results from further estigations, she will then ve at a definitive gnosis and instigate propriate treatment.

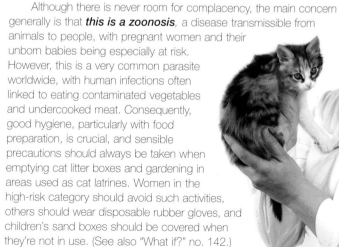

What if my cat doesn't like going to the vet?

124

Few of us really like going to the doctor or hospital, but some pets dread the experience, becoming warier as time goes by if there are signs that such a trip is imminent. Therefore, it pays to be proactive in reducing the stress associated with veterinary visits.

Always have a dedicated carrier that's appropriate to your pet's size; never rely on readily available household items, like bags, or a cardboard box that's only suitable for kittens. If you struggle to keep your cat in his container, or it breaks, he's going to be highly aroused before you reach your destination, clinical examination will be more difficult and less meaningful, and the results of some tests may be less reliable than if the patient is calm.

Whether you use a plastic carrier or wicker basket, ensure by having it out all the time that it doesn't become a "signal" that puts your cat "on alert." Make it an attractive place for your pet to "hang out" so it smells reassuring. Choosing a style that's suitable (with the top or door removed) to use as his bed is ideal. Place a blanket inside and hide toys and treats there for your cat to find and enjoy, thereby creating positive associations so that when you need to transport him he's less upset by being enclosed in his container. You can reduce stress even further by occasionally shutting him in the carrier briefly when nothing untoward happens, and ahead of your journey spraying the interior with commercial pheromone, or rubbing the interior with a towel or blanket containing his own reassuring social scents.

When you do go out, cover the basket/box with a cloth that smells familiar or has been sprayed with pheromones, because cats calm down more quickly in the dark, and it's alarming for them to see the world passing by. Anchor your pet's blanket and his carrier firmly, so he doesn't slip around, and obviously drive slowly and carefully to minimize the trauma of the journey.

On arrival, consider staying in the car if your wait will be prolonged or if your cat has previously had negative experiences with the clinic or is newly rescued. Staff can let you know when the vet or nurse is ready for you. If you sit in the waiting room:

- Choose a quiet area if cat-only space isn't provided.
- Keep your cat covered up.
- Place him in an elevated position, for example on a shelf, chair, or stool to help keep him calm.
- Protect him from intrusion by other people and pets, especially dogs.
- Talk calmly and quietly to reassure, but don't open the basket to comfort him—it's a security risk.

Once in the consulting room, tell the veterinarian why you're there, and give your pet time to adjust before getting him out. Make sure he's gently lifted, not pulled, then place another towel on the examination table so your cat has something familiar to sit on but is not additionally worried by his own stress pheromones that may be on the blanket he's traveled on.

Reverse the process on the way home. Don't hang around waiting for further appointments and medications with your cat at floor level in a busy walkway. If you have to wait, pop him out to your vehicle or ask to sit in another quiet area until you can leave.

Above: *Finding a truly cat-friendly vet makes clinic visits much less stressful for everyone!*

What if my cat won't take a tablet or let me apply ointment or put drops in his ears?

125

Dosing cats is a notoriously difficult area of human activity! However, manufacturers are now producing feline-friendly products. Palatable medicines and tablets, ointments in easy-to-use containers, and new style "pill poppers" make such tasks less problematic for us and unpleasant for our pets. Ask your vet for cat-friendly preparations, and request demonstration of techniques for administering oral formulations and applying ointments or ear preparations effectively. Practice makes perfect, but you'll be more confident and get more cooperation from your cat if you know how to do the job properly. It also helps to associate the procedure with something nice, like a very tasty food treat or game, immediately afterwards.

What if my cat is neutered?

126

Qualified veterinarians neuter cats under general anaesthetic. Males are castrated, while in the female ovariohysterectomy (spaying) is performed.

Castration: Both testicles are removed from the scrotum through an incision made in the skin. It rarely requires stitches and heals quickly so long as the cat leaves the wound alone post-operatively. In some cats one or both testes fails to descend into the scrotum from the abdominal cavity, where they are at birth. The surgeon must locate them in the groin or perform an abdominal operation if they've not even reached that far. These are more involved procedures but recovery is generally uncomplicated.

Advantages: Castration has two main functions. It prevents breeding and eliminates the effects of the sex hormones, which diminishes the characteristic "muscling up" of the mature tom and the smell associated with his urine, which most people find difficult to live with. The male's desire to roam, advertise his presence by spraying urine, and fight rivals for "mating rights" over sexually active queens is also diminished. This is important because intact (i.e., unneutered) males are not only more prone to those diseases transmitted through bites, such as FIV, but they also appear to be involved in more road traffic accidents and are at greater risk of getting lost in unfamiliar territory than neutered pets.

above: After spaying, some cats are sensitive around their operation site. Ask your vet about an Elizabethan collar, which will help to stop your pet from introducing infection to her surgical wound or removing her sutures.

Spaying: Removal of the ovaries and uterus (womb) is done either through a flank or midline incision. Cats are remarkably resilient, and the benefits of modern anaesthetics and analgesics (pain killers) mean that they're usually back to normal after a few days, although some have to wear an Elizabethan collar to stop them chewing their stitches, introducing infection, or making the skin around the wound sore.

Advantages: Spaying controls reproduction with the added advantages that tom cats don't hang around whenever the queen is in season, and your pet cannot later be troubled by pyometra (infection of the uterus) or neoplasia (cancer) of the ovaries and uterus.

Post-operative conditions: When neutered both sexes put on weight more readily and become indolent if owners fail to control their food intake and ensure they keep active. You can help your cat avoid these problems by paying attention to his or her nutrition and encouraging exercise.

What if my cat isn't neutered?

127

Neutering is routinely done before or just after the onset of sexual maturity. Puberty occurs at around five to six months of age, depending upon breed and sex; pedigree cats are sometimes precocious, and males tend to mature later than queens.

Females are **seasonally polyestrous,** which means they have breeding seasons at certain times of year, influenced by day length, so most kittens are born in spring and summer. Between seasons they spurn advances from males, but during "heat" or "calling cycles" their behavior changes. They show receptivity and willingness to mate by urinary spraying and typical vocal yowling; often they become more affectionate and roll around on the ground, apparently writhing in pain, before adopting a mating posture, known as "lordosis." This period lasts about five days unless the queen is mated, in which case the male's withdrawing his barbed penis causes an egg to be released and fertilized, termed "induced ovulation." The cycle continues in the unmated female every three weeks until the end of the breeding season about three months later.

Above: Mating is usually a speedy affair, after which the queen stops calling and the local toms quickly lose interest in her.

The **gestation period** is around 63 days, with up to six kittens being the norm. The queen's nutritional requirements increase during pregnancy, although it's important she doesn't gain too much weight and keeps active until the last stages. As soon as you think your pet may be pregnant, consult your vet for advice about management during this important stage and how to handle her offsprings' birth.

Contraception is available in tablet and injectable forms, but such drugs are not without their potential risks, such as the development of **pyometra.** This condition, where the uterus fills with pus, also occurs naturally in unspayed queens and is a good reason to consider hysterectomy (surgical removal of the uterus) as a preventive measure. Spaying is the only treatment, without which the toxicity caused by this hormonally dependent condition is fatal. Sometimes an offensive, mucky discharge exudes from the vagina, although this doesn't always happen, which makes diagnosis more difficult. Other signs include:

* Anorexia
* Increased thirst
* Depression
* Vomiting

If you see any such signs in your unneutered female, ***take her immediately to your veterinary clinic.***

Above: Changes in drinking patterns and increases in thirst warrant a veterinary visit.

White or yellowish discharges that sometimes occur in spayed cats indicate **vaginitis** (inflammation and infection of the vagina), which unlike pyometra is not life-threatening. Don't delay a visit to your vet, though, because the sooner appropriate treatment is instigated, the better.

What if my cat won't eat?

128

If your cat goes off his food, don't panic, but don't ignore the fact either. If the anorexia is associated with other clinical signs, head straight to your veterinarian. Otherwise look around to make sure your pet isn't stressed by something in the environment. For example, have there been any upsets in your home, say stressful work-related incidents, a burglary or bereavement, construction work, unfamiliar visitors staying, a new baby or pet arriving, or a prized human companion going away. If the answer is "Yes," you probably need to concentrate on creating a reassuring environment and predictable timetable to help your pet settle down again.

However, in the absence of an obvious stressor, a visit to your vet should help decide if the reduced food intake is caused by appetite loss or difficulty/inability to eat or swallow. You can aid diagnosis by providing tasty morsels that your pet usually craves, warming his food to make it more appetizing, and tempting him to eat while observing any signs of discomfort or difficulty. But if these measures fail to improve the situation quickly or your pet is off color, note the onset of the behavioral change and any other signs, and visit your veterinary clinic.

What if my cat tries to eat but hisses at his food, drops it as if he's been stung by a bee, runs away, or claws at his mouth?

129

This generally indicates discomfort or pain associated with the mouth. Problems can involve teeth, gums, tongue, or throat. If your cat behaves this way, wrap him in a towel, like a barber's robe, so he can't scratch you, and gently examine his mouth. Have tweezers handy so you can carefully remove anything that's stuck, such as a piece of bone wedged along the top of his teeth or between them, a trapped fish bone, or even a piece of twig, grass or leaf if he's been chewing plants. Otherwise, look for a broken or loose tooth, wounds, inflamed gums (gingivitis), ulcers, or infection, which will probably make your pet's breath smell unpleasant (halitosis). However, unless the problem is straightforward and easily remedied, ***don't delay getting your vet's help.*** Even if a loose tooth that you've removed caused the behavior, don't overlook a veterinary check, because gum disease (periodontal disease) is common in cats. Your pet may require more radical treatment, including scaling and polishing his teeth to remove plaque. This is important, because a number of diseases affecting the major organs, heart, liver, and kidneys, can arise from undetected dental infections.

Preventive Care: Whatever your cat's age, your vet will also advise you about routine home treatments to prevent dental disease. It's wise to introduce the "art" of teeth cleaning when you first get your kitten. If you've missed this opportunity, try the procedure with your adult pet, provided he's easily handled so you don't get scratched or accidentally brush his gums. There's a range of equipment, including tiny brushes and palatable toothpastes, designed to help, but if the task proves impossible, consider a commercial dental diet, which has a more abrasive texture than normal dry cat food, or dental chew sticks designed to remove tartar. (See also "What if?" no. 123—cat flu, chlamydophila, FIV.)

What if my cat dribbles?

130

Some cats dribble out of contentment, so context is crucial. If your cat is fit and well but commonly dribbles when sitting on your knee purring happily, don't worry! On the other hand, if his saliva is more profuse than normal, smells foul, is thick or blood-tinged, or if he's reluctant to eat or off color, suspect problems with his mouth or throat. These can relate to local lesion say an infected wound, or systemic disease, such as cat flu, which cause ulcers. In summer it's possible he's been stung inside his mouth by a bee or wasp, so your cat's face may also be externally swollen.

Examine him in case he needs first aid, then contact your clinic. Deep sedation or a general anaesthetic may be needed to locate and deal with cause of the problem, followed by antibiotic treatment. (See also "What if? no.123—cat flu, chlamydophila, FIV.)

What if my cat eats but has difficulty swallowing?

131

Below: Act quickly if your cat uncharacteristically dribbles or has difficulty swallowing or closing his mouth.

Gagging and gulping, which become more obvious when he's trying to swallow food or saliva, are gene the clue when a cat has:

- an infected throat with swelling and/or ulceration of tissues, including lymph glands.
- a bit of bone stuck across his pharynx.
- a blade of grass working its way up into the nasal cavity by curling arou the hard palate (roof of the mouth).

Upper respiratory infections can also cause this behavior, as can penetrat foreign bodies, for instance fish hooks, sewing needles, sharp fragments stick, or in some areas strong grass awns which can penetrate skin and mucous membrane. Such organic foreign bodies are especially problematic because once lodged in tissues, they don't show up X-rays like metal objects, so locating and removing them can be difficult. In addition, vital blood vessels and nerves around the hea and neck are vulnerable to something traveling through tissues tak infection with it, so **don't delay getting veterinary help** if your c has this sort of problem.

It's also important when owners enjoy craftwork to ensure that pins, needles, and other shiny, sharp tools are stored out of reach of pets Curiosity can indeed kill cats that are attracted by thread or wool attached to needles, play with it, and quickly swallow the lot! Some cats manage to pass needles safely through their intestinal tracts, bu there's always the risk of one getting stuck, causing life-threatening damage and/or requiring major abdominal surgery to remove it.

In fact, a range of household items can potentially cause such problems, especially when bored cats seek out inappropriate playthings because they lack attractive, legitimate items to play and as an outlet for normal predatory behavior. Thus owners shc always provide ideal facilities for their cats, while taking care to remove potentially harmful objects from their reach. (See also "Wh ifs?" nos. 123—cat flu, chlamydophila—139, 140, and 148.)

What if my cat sneezes or has a runny nose and weepy eyes?

132

The severity of these signs is important, whether or not your pet is also off color, has a diminished appetite, or is coughing; so too is the context in which they occur. If your cat has been "helping" you clean a dusty corner, or the pollen count is high, he may just be suffering from irritation of his eyes and the mucous membranes of his upper respiratory system or a mild bout of hay fever.

However, if he's unwell, the discharges are mucky, his eyelids are swollen, one or both eyes are closed, or he is coughing, **take him straight to the vet**. It may be that just rest and TLC (tender loving care) are needed to shake off a virus, but antibiotics are sometimes necessary to deal with more serious bacterial complications. And if he's contracted a more major disease, the sooner your pet gets medical attention, the better his chances of uneventful recovery will be. (See also "What if?" no. 123—cat flu, chlamydophila.)

What if my cat has a closed and swollen eye?

133

Never take chances with eyes; they're precious! If you cannot clearly see your cat's eyeball because of swelling, prompt veterinary attention is required. Facial injuries are common after cat fights, and these may lead to painful abscesses. These can cause considerable tissue damage, and systemic infections may subsequently develop. They need lancing, draining, and flushing under sedation, and antibiotics are usually prescribed, even if abscesses burst naturally.

Other possibilities in this situation are penetrating foreign bodies, for example a sharp grass awn working its way into the eyelid, or a wound to the eyeball itself. The cornea (clear part of the eye) is vulnerable to bumps and scratches, which can quickly become infected. Gently bathe your pet's eye in warm water while waiting for your veterinary appointment, but **speed is important here**, so don't waste time. (See also "What if?" no. 123.)

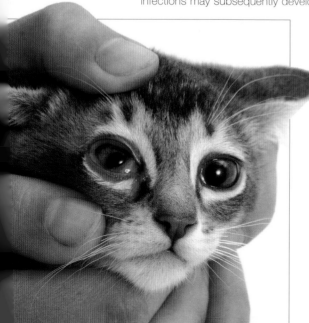

Left: Fluorescein, an orange dye, is often used by veterinarians to detect corneal ulcers and to determine how serious they are.

What if my cat has a red eyeball?

134

Cats' eyes are vulnerable to trauma from falls, fight and road traffic accidents, so they can sometimes get "black eyes." You may see other signs, such a scuffed claws, a limp, or more serious injuries, which require the vet to check your pet over.

However, if your cat's eyeball fills with blood, he is suffering an intra-ocular hemorrhage. *This is an emergency requiring immediate action.* may indicate that your pet has dangerously high blood pressure, a consequence of which can be retinal detachment and blindness. Older pe are particularly at risk and should be checked regularly, as reliable treatmen for this condition are generally available despite blood pressure monitoring not yet being routine in general veterinary practice. *Early detection is highly desirable because it allows preemptive action to be taken.* (S also "What if?" no. 156.)

What if my cat is coughing or has labored breathing?

135

Cats commonly cough briefly if something irritates their throats, but if your pet's cough is more seriou take him for a checkup.

This will be an emergency situation if he is suffering from sever respiratory embarrassment (dyspnea) with panting, his chest and/o abdomen is pumping, his neck is extended, and the mucous membranes of his mouth are very pale or tinged with blue.

If this happens:
- Telephone to ensure veterinary staff are ready with oxygen on hand.
- Make sure there's no obvious obstruction in his throat or affecting his nose, then handle your cat as little as possible.
- Put him in a quiet, darkened, well-ventilated room, and keep other pets and people away.
- Transport him as gently as the urgency of the situation allows.
- Note the time of onset and any pertinent facts that may help w diagnosis, such as where your pet was when the problem started.

Once stabilized, your cat may need quite extensive investigati using blood tests, X-rays, and ultrasound to diagnose the underlyi problem, because a range of conditions affecting the respiratory a cardiovascular systems, especially the lungs and heart, can cause these signs. They include:
- Complications associated with cat flu, such as pneumonia.
- Pleurisy—infection of the lining of the chest, which results in fluid accumulation.
- Asthma.
- Tumors.
- Foreign bodies.
- Traumatic events, for example traffic accidents or falls, which sometime result in a rupture of the diaphragm, hemothorax (blood in the chest cavity), or pneumothorax (air in the chest cavity). (See also "What ifs?" nos. 114, 117, 120, 135, 147, 155, and 156.)

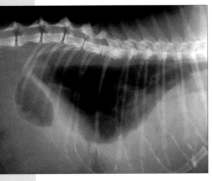

Above: *Blood tests and X- rays are commonly used to diagnose heart and lung problems.*

What if my cat has mucky, smelly ears?

136

Feline ears are usually clean and sweet-smelling. So if your cat:
- produces excess wax—blackish brown moist/crusty deposits
- scratches his ears
- hangs his head on one side
- has smelly ears with a purulent creamy discharge . . . he is likely to be suffering from otitis externa, an infection of the outer ear.

Mites, tiny parasites that irritate the skin lining the ear canal and cause inflammation, are another common cause, but bacterial and fungal infections also occur. Don't do more than gently wipe loose or liquid debris away with a tissue. Arrange to go to the clinic, where your vet will look into your pet's ear canals with an auroscope, diagnose the problem, and prescribe an appropriate treatment. Ask for a demonstration if applying eardrops (**left**) is a skill you've yet to acquire! (See also "What if?" no. 137.)

What if my cat has a swollen ear?

137

The tissues of the pinna, the external part of the ear, may swell up if a wasp or bee stings your cat. Alternatively, if his whole ear is soft and puffy he could have an abscess or hematoma, which occurs when a blood vessel ruptures between the two flaps of cartilage that form the ear. If untreated eventually the blood "organizes," with the tissues crumpling into a "cauliflower ear." Obviously, veterinary attention is needed, but you can help initially by locating and bathing any fight wound or using a cold compress on a sting.

Cats with white ears—especially in hot countries—are vulnerable to skin cancer, squamous cell carcinoma, which often starts as crusty scabs around the edge of the pinna. There may be irritation and bleeding if this serious problem goes untreated. So if your cat is in a high-risk category, take preemptive action by using sun block on his ears to prevent sunburn in fine weather, and consult your vet immediately you notice any suspicious changes. (See also "What if?" no. 106.)

bove: Regularly examine ur cat's ears so you will otice immediately if things e going wrong.

What if my cat has a swelling around his face?

138

A range of problems—both internal and external—can cause swellings in the facial area. For instance:

- ticks
- infected bite wounds
- insect stings
- tooth root abscesses
- tumors of the skin or deeper tissues, including facial bones

This is why it's important to examine your cat carefully on a regular basis to ensure you spot any early changes and **consult your vet quickly if you do.** (See also "What ifs?" nos. 62, 63, 128, 129, 130, and 131.)

What if my cat eats grass or plants?

139

Many cats naturally eat grass as a form of roughage, a habit that may increase if they feel nauseous or otherwise off-color. This is nothing to worry about unless your cat seems unwell. Then you should note other signs and consult your veterinarian.

However, some pets, especially those kept indoors all the time, put themselves at risk by eating the leaves of indoor plants and cut flowers, a surprising number of which are toxic to our cats. These include:

- Lilies
- Amaryllis
- Chrysanthemum
- Cyclamen
- Ferns
- Holly
- Poinsettia
- Ivy
- Laburnum

It's important therefore to ensure that cats have plenty of other things with which to amuse themselves and satisfy their curiosity, and to avoid

Above: Some respected feline charities have lists on their Web sites of plants and flowers that are poisonous to cats, so owners can check before introducing anything new into their homes or gardens.

introducing poisonous greenery into our homes and gardens that poses a threat to the well-being of our pets. (See also "What ifs?" nos. 34, 95, 130, 131, 135, 142, 155.)

Right: Youngsters are especially curious. If you have a kitten, take extra care.

What if my cat vomits?

140

Cats regurgitate food and vomit for a variety of reasons. They can eat too much grass, something may disagree with them, or they may need to get rid of "fur balls"—excess fur that they've ingested during grooming. Allergies, infections, foreign bodies, toxic substances, gastric ulceration, tumors, and other diseases of the major organs, such as the liver, also cause vomiting.

Note any other unusual signs and behavior, how long after eating your pet regurgitates his food, whether he is having trouble swallowing, and if he can still keep down water. If your cat is otherwise well, telephone the clinic to ask about home care, which may include a short period of light food and observation. On the other hand, if he's depressed, has diarrhea, or is not eating, make an appointment without delay.

Also ensure you regularly groom your pet's coat, particularly if he's long-haired or has difficulty keeping his coat in good condition himself. Even short-haired pets may need additional brushing when they shed excessively because of high temperatures or because your heating is on in cold weather. (See also "What ifs?" nos. 123, 127—pyometra, 130, 131, 142, 147, 148, 149, 151, 155, and 156.)

Above: Owners have an important role to play in a cat's coat maintenance.

What if my cat drags his bottom along the ground?

141

Cats' "trousers" sometimes get knotted, and feeling uncomfortable, they skid along the floor on their bottoms. So, particularly with longer fur, it's important to ensure their hind legs are well groomed with no evidence of fecal matting or soreness, because this could attract flies in hot weather. If they lay eggs around a pet's bottom, the hatching maggots can burrow into skin and underlying tissues, causing damage and severe toxicity, *an urgent veterinary case that's easy to avoid with good management at home.*

Other reasons for this behavior are:

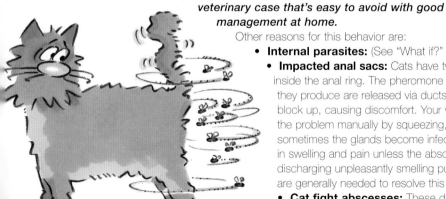

- **Internal parasites:** (See "What if?" no. 142.)
- **Impacted anal sacs:** Cats have two small sacs inside the anal ring. The pheromone secretions they produce are released via ducts that can block up, causing discomfort. Your vet will relieve the problem manually by squeezing, but sometimes the glands become infected, resulting in swelling and pain unless the abscess bursts, discharging unpleasantly smelling pus. Antibiotics are generally needed to resolve this problem.
- **Cat fight abscesses:** These develop when cats run from opponents, but not quickly enough! Puncture wounds from the other cat's canine teeth fester, so check his hindquarters carefully for telltale signs if your cat is involved in a fight. Bathe small wounds with warm water, but seek your vet's advice for anything more substantial or if your pet seems off color.

What if my cat has diarrhea?

142

This can be the only sign that a cat is passing loose feces if he's otherwise well. Therefore, if you can't find any other indicators, keep your pet inside with a litter box to check what he's producing. If there's anything abnormal about his excreta, take a sample with you when you visit the clinic.

Generally with diarrhea, cats pass stools more frequently, feces are loose, and the color may be abnormal. Pets may be otherwise well, with the problem only coming to light when they drag their bottoms, noticeably lose weight and/or their third eyelids (the "haws") come up across the eyes from the inner corner as if a skin is growing over their eyeballs. (See also "What ifs?" nos. 119, 121, 122, 141, 143, and 148.)

Diarrhea has a variety of causes:
- **Inappropriate diet**, for example milk in adult cats.
- **Food allergy**.
- **Infections**—bacterial and viral.
- **Internal parasites**—worms, toxoplasma, giardia (a single-celled parasite often associated with poor hygiene, which is passed between cats via infected feces).
- **Tumors**.
- **Foreign body ingestion or intussusception** (a problem with the intestine where one portion telescopes or prolapses into an adjoining section).
- **Drug reactions**.
- **Endocrine disease** such as hyperthyroidism.

Above: *Unusually seeing your cat's third eyelids could indicate he has an upset digestive tract.*

Above: *The* Taenia *tapeworm uses these suckers to attach itself to the host cat.*

Right: *A* Dipylidium caninum *tapeworm. Your vet is the best source of advice about the ideal regular worming regime*

Common Internal Parasites
- **Roundworm**—sometimes seen in stools or when a pet vomits.
- **Tapeworm**—may be seen as small segments in feces, around your cat's bottom, or as "grains of rice" where he's been sitting.
- **Lungworm**—sometimes a cause of coughing in cats; detection requires special tests.
- **Whipworm, hookworm, and heartworm**—they are not present everywhere. If yours is an infected area, or you plan to move or travel with your cat, ask your vet about preventive treatments.

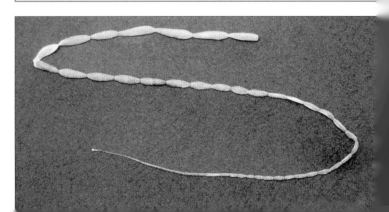

What if my cat passes blood and/or mucus in his feces?

143 Mucus can look like slime, jelly, or a skin covering feces, which may be loose; it generally indicates a problem associated with the large bowel (colon). Dietary sensitivities, parasites, infections, and stress can all cause this condition, so you may need the help of your vet plus a behaviorist if your cat's well-being is in question. (See also "What ifs?" nos. 25 and 142.)

What if my cat is constipated?

144 Spotting this is easier with an indoor cat, where the signs are absence of stools in the litter box and no inappropriate elimination! Sometimes dry and hard feces are passed, with a cat straining more than usual.

Constipation can be a particular problem in elderly pets, following surgery or an accident that results in pelvis injuries, or after a cat has eaten bones and feathers or ingested excess fur. The latter is another reason to groom your pet, especially when he's shedding a lot of fur. It also makes sense to avoid inappropriate raw food diets and to discourage hunting, if you can.

Below: Check if your cat licks his rear end excessively. He may just need help with fur matts, but call your vet quickly if you suspect a more serious condition.

Despite the many laxatives on the market, if your cat is constipated, ask advice from your veterinary staff before administering anything. It may not be suitable for your pet, who could require an enema, which only a veterinarian should administer. Additionally, if the problem recurs, dietary manipulation with increased fiber or stool softeners may be needed.

Beware—if your male cat strains, don't assume he's constipated. Tomcats are susceptible to urethral obstruction. The urethra, which conveys urine from the bladder when a cat relieves himself, is narrow and travels around a bend. This anatomy makes it vulnerable to blockage from crystal sediment and mucous plugs that sometimes collect in the bladder. The behavior of a male with this problem can be indistinguishable from that of a constipated cat, with agitated hole digging, straining, sniffing, and licking of the hindquarters, belly, and penis, which is often bruised or sore as a result.

This is an emergency situation requiring immediate veterinary intervention to relieve the blockage by catheterization under sedation/general anaesthetic, followed by investigation and treatment of the underlying cause. Long-term management of the problem may rely on special diets, although sometimes surgical incision of a stricture of the urethra (perineal urethrotomy) is required. This surgery creates a permanent bypass, thereby making the male's anatomy not unlike that of the female, where the urethra is shorter and straighter. (See also "What ifs?" nos. 139, 140, 147, 149, and 151.)

What if my cat starts to eat more than normal?

145

Always feed a balanced diet that's suitable for you cat's age. Kittens and elderly pets have special needs, and we now have a range of specialized formulations to help manage specific feline diseases. Remember, cats are obligate carnivores, meaning they must have meat and cannot become vegetarian. Otherwise, lack of taurine, an essential amino acid found only in flesh, causes irreversible blindness. Take care also that your cat doesn't develop a passion for certain items; excess vitamin A in liver, for instance, causes crippling arthritis.

Naturally, if your cat becomes more active than normal, his appetite will increase. But obesity is now a major problem, which reflects more sedentary feline lifestyles, good quality nutrition, and overindulgence by owners, who too often show affection with food! The approach to this aspect of management is behavioral as well as medical, with measured calorie intake balanced by increased exercise; encourage your cats to play, and let them forage for food rather than get it "for free." Remember, your pet may put on weight more read after neutering and as he matures; weigh him regularly, and seek veterinary advice if he gains too much.

However, a number of conditions, which generally affect older cats, can cause an increased appetite that ofte coincides with drinking more, sometimes losing weight or changing body shape. If you notice anything suspicious, consult your veterinarian. Fecal, urine, and blood tests will be necessa to look, among other things, for the following conditions:

- Intestinal parasites
- Other causes of diarrhea
- Kidney disease
- Liver disease
- Diabetes mellitus
- Hyperthyroidism
- Tumors

(See also "What ifs?" nos. 43, 123, 127, 142, 146, and 156.)

What if my cat is drinking more and/or passing more urine than normal?

146

Conditions described in "What if?" no. 145 can additionally cause increased thirst with resultant urine production, which may be the first sign that something is wrong. If your pet starts drinking more, particularly if he's a "senior," monitor his intake and overall behavior, and take him to your vet. (See also "What if?" no. 21.)

Right: Some cats regularly drink from running taps, but when it's unusual, suspect a problem.

What if my cat looks pregnant but is a male or neutered female?

Right: Never ignore changes in your cat's shape. If he's getting fatter, check with your vet before you decrease his food intake and increase his exercise.

147 A number of conditions are associated with changes in the shape of a cat's abdomen. This should **never be ignored**, especially when appearing in connection with other suspicious signs. Obviously, the belly may simply swell because a pet has overindulged, so gas accumulates as digestion proceeds. However, acsites (fluid collection in the abdomen) can be a consequence of some serious conditions involving the cardio-vascular system or liver, for instance. And the lymph glands associated with the intestines are a common site for tumor development in older cats, particularly those infected with FeLV. So, if your cat looks unexpectedly pregnant, pay attention to the other important signs, such as thirst and appetite (increased or reduced), lethargy, or breathing difficulty, and take him for a checkup. Your pet may need blood and urine tests, X-ray, or ultrasound to diagnose the problem. (See also "What ifs?" nos. 123, 140, 142, and 156.)

What if my cat eats wool or fabric or licks plastic bags or concrete?

148 Ingesting soft foreign objects can lead to ulceration of the intestinal tract, its obstruction, or intussusception, where the gut concertinas on itself. **These can all be life-threatening conditions requiring surgery** that is potentially complicated. Obviously, "prevention is better than cure." Therefore, particularly if your cat is in a high-risk category for developing compulsive disorders associated with wool/fabric chewing, examine your environment and management to reduce his motivation for the behavior.

Pica: Abnormal cravings for unusual substances can lead cats to lick concrete or stones, for instance. It can be associated with metabolic imbalances from developing diseases and so warrants a trip to your vet, particularly when it is observed in "senior" pets. (See also "What ifs?" nos. 33, 50, 145, and 156.)

Left: Cats normally investigate anything new in their environment. But if your pet starts chewing potentially harmful objects or fabrics, never laugh or get cross; try to work out why it is happening and do something constructive about it.

What if my cat is scratching and/or licking himself more than normal?

149

Examine your cat's fur regularly and help him to keep it trim, especially if he's long-haired, elderly, or arthritic. Then you'll be well acquainted with normality and quickly spot signs of:

- Hair loss—which may be widespread or affect only a small area
- Redness
- Soreness
- Scabs
- Crusts
- Wounds
- Discharges, such as pus
- Bleeding
- Lumps—these may affect all layers of the skin and areas of the body, being superficial, soft, and regular in outline or firmer and more problematic. They range from ticks, abscesses, and benign fluid-filled cysts, through penetrating foreign bodies, to cancers and the occasional air gun pellet.

Some minor problems you may deal with yourself. For example, fur mats can be carefully cut out with blunt-ended scissors after placing a precautionary comb in the base of the hair next to the skin to prevent accidental injury. Afterwards, tease out the base of the knotted hair. Small wounds may respond to warm dilute saline bathing. Try to stop your cat licking sore areas, and avoid applying ointment, which will only attract his attention, until your vet has prescribed appropriate treatment.

External parasites: Insects that live on or in the superficial layers of the skin and survive by sucking a pet's blood are one of the most widespread causes of these signs.

Above: The cat flea is the intermediate host for the common tapeworm Dipylidium caninum.

The Most Common External Parasites

Fleas

As adults they are visible to the naked eye, appearing as tiny, hopping creatures when you part your cat's fur. Some pets become highly allergic to them (as do some humans) and can suffer severe self-inflicted trauma to their skin as a result of irritation.

So regular flea control is part of good management. A variety of products is available, some of which combine internal (intestinal worm) and external parasite control and deal with the problem of environmental contamination with flea eggs. You can choose between:

- Special flea collars
- Sprays
- Powders
- Shampoos
- "Spot-on" products
- Preparations available from veterinarians are usually more effective than "over-the-counter" versions from pet shops. And if your cat

Above: Cats get sore skin when irritation from lice makes them itchy.

Above: Some sensitive owners develop rashes when Cheyletiella mites affect their cats.

Above: Ringworm isn't always obvious. Consult your vet at once if your cat has contact with infected animals.

becomes infested, you also need to pay attention to reducing the eggs, larvae, and pupal stages that can build up in your home, particularly in hot weather or when your heating is on, when hatching is rapid. Ask advice about a coherent management strategy to deal effectively with the problem and to prevent recurrence.

Lice

These are not common in cats, but where they occur, their whole life cycle is lived on the animal. They glue their eggs (nits) onto the hair, and, although small, both adults and nits are visible to us. Get your vet's advice about treatment.

Ticks

These globular insects attach very firmly to the skin using their biting mouthparts. Their colors range from fawn to slate gray, and starting very small they swell by engorging themselves on the animal's blood. Eventually they fall off to lie in wait for the next feeding season, but they can cause significant local inflammation.

Single ticks suddenly appearing on any area of cats' bodies are easily mistaken for chewing gum or warts, though it's not uncommon to find numbers of them, particularly around the face or legs.

It is not advisable to attempt removal unless you have been shown exactly what to do, because it's easy to leave part of the insect behind, giving rise to local infections. Occasionally ticks carry blood-borne diseases, such as Lyme's disease.

Some flea preparations also provide protection against ticks, and your veterinary staff will know if they are common in your locality.

Mites

These microscopic insects can live on the skin's surface or in the hair follicles. They usually cause dandruff and irritation. In fact one of them, *Cheyletiella*, is sometimes referred to as "walking dandruff."

Veterinarians microscopically examine coat brushings and skin scrapings to determine the species involved in mite infestations before prescribing appropriate treatment.

Ringworm

This is actually a fungal disease that causes circular lesions, mainly around the face, head, and forelegs, and most commonly in young cats. But it may be asymptomatic (i.e., not producing any symptoms) and does not always cause irritation. It's very easily passed between pets, is transmissible to humans, and can be troublesome to deal with when spores have contaminated the environment, so ***go straight to your vet*** if you have any suspicions. Oral treatments, washes, shampoos, and ointments are used as well as hair clipping.

(See also "What ifs?" nos. 58 and 122.)

What if my cat licks his belly until it's bald?

150

Your veterinarian needs to check him for external parasites and other skin conditions, and also for feline lower urinary tract disease (FLUTD). Over-grooming the belly is frequently the only sign of this complex, and as yet not well understood, condition. Infections, stones, or tumors of the bladder can cause FLUTD and require medical investigations and treatment.

However, many cases fall into the category of Feline Idiopathic Cystitis (FIC), that is, their cause is unidentified, although a clear link between this condition and stress is established. Anxious cats and those in multi-cat and indoor-only homes are often most at risk as are sedentary, overweight, middle-aged individuals. Therefore, this is another condition where the solution is a combined veterinary and behavioral approach. (See also "What ifs?" nos. 58 and 151.)

What if my cat has difficulty passing urine?

151

Both sexes need to go to the veterinarian if they are observed straining and only passing small quantities of urine or none at all. *But in the male this is an emergency, because although this behavior can be seen with cystitis only veterinary investigation can distinguish between this and urethral obstruction.* (See also "What ifs?" nos. 21, 144, and 150.)

What if my cat is limping?

152

Lameness can vary in severity and cause. Cats pull muscles, sprain joints and ligaments, or fracture bones as a result of accidents. They're also susceptible to bite wound infections, inflammatory reactions in their joints, and degenerative joint diseases such as arthritis.

Onset may be abrupt, for instance after a fall or traffic accident, with obvious swelling, pain, and inflammation accompanying abnormal gait and loss of weight-bearing ability, or more gradual. If your pet is in distress, or shows evidence of shock, collapse, or other injuries, **this is an emergency requiring immediate medical attention.** Otherwise, examine him carefully to see if the problem is something relatively minor that you can deal with, for example, a small fight wound that needs bathing.

Also check your pet's claws, because especially in less mobile, elderly or disabled cats they can become too long and ingrown. Then tissues of the adjacent pads become inflamed and infected, a painful condition that can also affect polydactyl cats (those with more than the usual number of toes). These felines have extra claws on the inside of their paws, most commonly at the front, although some have one or even two additional toes on all four legs. Because they don't wear down, these extra claws can grow very long.

If your cat falls into any of these risk categories, ask your vet to demonstrate safe clipping so you can trim his claws regularly to avoid problems. (See also "What ifs?" nos. 112, 117, 119, 121, 126, 128, 133 and 135.)

Above: *Pain may make your cat untypically aggressive, so make sure you handle him carefully.*

What if my cat starts holding his head on one side so his neck is twisted?

...ght: Act quickly if your ...'s balance or head ...sition changes.

153 Cats can suffer from middle ear disease, which affects their balance, sometimes as a result of untreated otitis externa (inflammation of the ear canal). They're also prone to "vestibular syndrome," which has a sudden onset and produces these signs. Its cause is as yet undiscovered, but treatment is available and recovery is often good. Older pets are also most at risk of stroke and tumors of the brain, so if you spot anything of this sort, don't delay in getting your cat to the clinic. (See also "What ifs?" nos.136 and 154.)

What if my cat wobbles and falls over?

154 General musculoskeletal weakness and frailty are common in elderly cats. So long as your veterinarian has checked for disease and pain, don't worry, although your general management may need to accommodate your pet's increasingly limited mobility and reduced energy levels.

Others causes of unsteady gait, weakness, and collapse include shock, accidents, poisoning, and acute infections, **so apply appropriate first aid and seek veterinary help.** (See also "What ifs?" nos. 114, 117, 118, 136, 139, and 156.)

What if my ...t seems to be having a fit?

...t: "First aid" intervention ...e life-saving in some ...nstances. Seek ...e if your cat seems ...having a fit. Your ...arian will tell ...hat ...gency ...res you ...d take and how ...o transport him ...surgery.

155 Convulsions are upsetting to witness, but fortunately cats themselves are unlikely to be aware of what's happening. The signs vary, but often disorientation is followed by collapse with paddling movements of the limbs, which may be quite rigidly extended as the pet lies on his side.

Epilepsy, ingestion of toxic substances, head trauma, and pathological conditions of the brain can cause such problems. Limited intervention is advisable if your cat suffers a seizure, but you can help by reducing the amount of stimulation his nervous system receives. So:

- Switch off radios, televisions, and electric lights.
- Close doors, windows, and curtains.
- Move anything on which your cat may hurt himself.
- Put down a blanket for him to rest on.
- Keep him warm but not too hot.
- **Telephone your vet for help.** Clearly describe how and when you found your pet, with details of any potential causes, such as recent use of chemicals around the home and yard.

What if my cat is elderly?

156

Senior pets, those cats more than eight to ten years old, are more susceptible to a range of problems and pathological conditions, but they're particularly prone to:

Diseases of main organs and systems:

- Cardiovascular
  - Heart
    - Hypertension (raised blood pressure)
    - Iliac thrombosis—when a clot lodges and cuts off the blood supply to the hindlegs. **This is a medical emergency**, because the condition is painful and life-threatening. Affected cats may vocalize; drag their hindlegs, which become cold, stiff, or flaccid; or collapse completely. Left untreated, these pets suffer and may eventually go into respiratory failure. Surgery is not generally successful, but medical treatments are improving all the time, although sadly sometimes the only kind option is euthanasia.
  - Liver   • Kidney   • Cancer

Endocrine disease, especially:

- Diabetes
- Hyperthyroidism—a condition where generally benign enlargement of the thyroid gland causes excess production of hormones, so everything goes into "overdrive." Consequently, personality changes, including over-activity and uncharacteristic aggression, weight loss, increased thirst, and diarrhea are seen. Once diagnosed, the condition can be managed by drug therapy, surgery, or occasionally treatment with radioactive iodine in specialist centers.

Regular checkups should ensure early signs are picked up, the necessary tests initiated, and medical, dietary and support treatments prescribed. Hence the importance of senior pet clinics now offered by many veterinarians. Of course, attendance doesn't mean signs won't come to light between times, therefore if you notice any strange or suspicious changes in your elderly cat's behavior, your best course of action is to book another appointment.

In addition, it has recently been discovered that aged cats are susceptible to an Alzheimer's-like condition referred to as Cognitive Dysfunction (CD). The signs include:

- Confusion
- Memory deterioration
- Disorientation
- "Personality change"
- Loss of house training, grooming, interest in others and life
- Changes in sleep patterns
- Vocalizing

As there's no specific test available, diagnosis depends upon eliminating and/or adequately treating other problems that could cause the behavioral changes. Currently we have no cure, but supplementing an affected cat's diet with antioxidants and initiating supportive management can be helpful

Above: *Regular check-ups help vets to get to know elderly patients well. Then they are more likely to spot changes owners may not have noticed.*

ensuring that such pets enjoy the best quality of life possible.
(See also "What ifs?" nos. 128–131, 134, 135, 138, 144-148, 152, 153, and 155. Refer also to Part 6.)

What if my cat needs to be put to sleep or dies at home?

157

Pet owners always hope that their beloved cat will die peacefully in his sleep at home, but sadly this is unusual. For most of us, making the decision that our feline companion is suffering, or his quality of life is no longer acceptable in his terms, is an essential part of responsible ownership. While undeniably hard, "letting go" is our last act of love and should always be an owner's decision, but veterinarians are there to help and advise.

Many are happy to perform the procedure—an injection into the blood stream that quickly stops the heart—in a pet's home. Some owners, though, prefer to take their cats to the clinic, where staff should always try to accommodate individual preferences by setting aside an appointment at a quiet time and allowing clients to wait with their pet in a private area, both before and after his demise.

It is also a matter of individual choice (local laws governing the disposal of bodies may exist in some areas) whether a cat is buried, either at home or in a special pet cemetery, or cremated. It's wise to consider this ahead of time, so everyone agrees on a course of action and you never regret decisions made when you were deeply distressed, especially if your pet's death was unexpected.

Left: Senior cats in the twilight of their days enjoy a better quality of life now than ever before.

Below: Letting go is never easy, but often it's the genuinely loving thing for an owner to do.

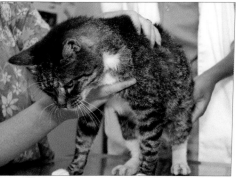

THE AGING CAT

PART 6

CONTENTS

What if my cat . . .

INTRODUCTION

Our pet cats are achieving fantastically long lives these days. Senior care is better than ever, and we now understand many of the conditions from which elderly cats suffer. It's estimated that about 30 percent of the cat population is actually classed as senior: senior cats are typically 8–10 years of age, and those reaching 15 years or more are considered geriatric. Luckily, many of us have the opportunity to share our lives with our cats for many years, and a little knowledge about the changes they are going through can help to make their later years easier and more pleasurable for them.

What if my cat is showing signs of senility?

158

Owners of elderly cats are often shocked to hear their cat is showing signs of mental deterioration. The condition is called **Feline Cognitive Dysfunction (FCD)** and is similar to Alzheimer's disease in humans. By the time they are classed as senior, many cats are actually starting to show some signs of cognitive decline, but others don't show any signs until they are in their late teens. Each cat will be affected differently, and there may be a range of indicators that alert you to the condition. (See also Part 5, "What if?" no. 156.)

If you recognize any of these symptoms and your cat is elderly, then seek advice from your vet. There are special diets and medications that can improve your cat's condition or at least slow down the onset of the deterioration.

Left: An elderly cat will begin to physically slow down but with the right care can be very content.

Feline—Human Age Comparison

Cat Age	Equivalent Human Years	Cat Age	Equivalent Human Years
1	15	11	60
2	24	12	64
3	28	13	68
4	32	14	72
5	36	15	76
6	40	16	80
7	44	17	84
8	48	18	88
9	52	19	92
10	56	20	96

What if my cat no longer sleeps on his normal bed?

159

Old cats do sleep for longer than young cats, but they also need to feel warm and secure. These cats often find an area away from drafts and as close to a fire or radiator as possible. Provide comfortable beds in places he can easily reach, since he may not be able to leap up high into his bed or might have problems jumping down when he awakens and feels stiff. Beds placed in boxes (with a side entry) can help to keep out the drafts, while foot stools and pet ramps can provide access to raised places. Some elderly cats seek warmth so much that they get too close to fires and may singe or burn themselves, so try to encourage him to use a cozy bed in a safe place. Be prepared to make a few adjustments to your home and routine to allow for your cat's changing abilities.

What if my cat is meowing loudly?

160

The reason for loud meowing may vary between individual cats. If your cat has always been vocal but the meows have recently become louder, it might be due to his hearing failing. Other cats who are beginning to show the signs of cognitive dysfunction may meow at times when they feel confused. They may feel disorientated when they wake up and often meow loudly until they locate their owner or the owner comes to them. If the vocalization has suddenly started, arrange for a veterinarian examination to rule out any pain or discomfort.

What if my cat doesn't groom like he used to?

161

As your cat gets older, it can become harder for him to keep up his previous grooming regime. Very elder and weak cats might begin to find even the simplest parts of their daily routine difficult to perform. Some cats that have become overweight stop grooming, because they can no longer bend and reach parts of their body. In this case you must discuss a diet plan with your vet, because obesity is linked to many other illnesses. Arthritis or mouth problems can deter your cat from attempting to groom. Your veterinarian wi be able to discuss these situations with you.

You will need to take charge of his grooming requirements so that his skin and coat remain in good condition. Without regular grooming, the oils in the coat won't be dispersed evenly and it will quickly become dull and scruffy. It's also useful to clip your cat's nails, because it's likely that an elderly cat won't wear them down enough through daily activity. Keeping them trimmed will be healthier and helps to prevent them from catching on you, your carpets, or bedding.

Above: *An old cat may soon begin to look unkempt.*

What if my cat has started to toilet in the wrong place?

162 Many older cats find it hard to climb into their litter boxes and so begin to toilet next to it. A surprising number of old cats suffer from hip and joint problems. However, cats are very good at hiding this problem, so don't expect to see an obvious limp. Old age also affects bladder control, and your cat may not be able to make it to the box in time. You should provide more litter boxes around the home so that he can always reach one quickly. A low-sided tray placed within a box set on its side, or a plastic storage box with one side cut out are both possible alternatives for an old cat who needs to access his toilet area easily. The fact that it has sides and is larger in area will help prevent accidents if your cat has trouble squatting properly.

What if my cat becomes deaf?

163 If your cat loses his hearing, you might have to make some changes to your daily routine. First signs are often that the cat seems easier to surprise or startle. This is often because they can no longer hear where you are and so feel anxious. Since deaf cats are easily startled if you walk up behind them or if awakened suddenly, it's best to try to make a vibration to warn him in advance of your presence. This can be done by stamping on the floor, closing a door, or dropping something on the floor. You might notice your cat becoming clingier around the home. A commercial collar is available if you worry that your cat may get lost or cannot come when you call him—it emits a noise when you activate it so *you can locate him yourself*.

If your cat still ventures outdoors, always check behind your car before turning the ignition, and ask your neighbors to be vigilant, because your cat will no longer get a warning when the engine starts and so is more likely to be involved in an accident.

What if my cat goes blind?

164 We are all aware that as we get older, eyesight tends to decline. This also happens with our cats. Be fair to him and try to keep his routine and environment consistent. Try not to rearrange your furniture too often, because your cat will be relying on familiarity to navigate his way around the house. Remember that your cat will not be able to see you coming and may not move out of your way; he will also not be able to react to warnings from other cats. Keep an eye out for bullying or for distress caused by other pets. Use your voice (if he still has his hearing) to help him locate you.

Right: With any cat with failing eyesight, it's helpful to create a routine and keep familiar items bearing its scent around the house, which will help him feel relaxed and aid his orientation.

INDEX

PICTURE CREDITS

Bayer HealthCare: 109 bottom left and center, 140 center left, 140 bottom, 144.

Jane Burton, Warren Photographic: 23 center left, 24 both, 25 both, 26 center left, 33 both, 34 top, 37 center right, 41 top, 41 bottom right, 42 bottom right, 45 top right, 45 bottom, 46 bottom, 47, 51, 57 top, 66 top, 70 top (cat), 77 bottom, 80 top, 82 top, 88, 90 both, 91, 92 top, 95 center, 97 bottom right, 123 bottom, 125 bottom, 127 top left, 128 top left, 129 top left, 132 top left, 133, 134 top left, 135, 137 top, 140 top left, 141, 145 bottom left, 146 top left, 147 both.

Interpet Archive: 44, 49 center, 61 bottom right, 66 bottom, 103 top right, 105 top right, 108, 131.

iStockphoto.com:
Terry Adams: 50. Gregory Albertini: 29 center right. Manon Allard: 142. Douglas Allen: 138 center. Andsem: 101 top. Stephanie Asher: 112 bottom. Irina Bachinskaya: 55 bottom, 93 bottom. Joe Belanger: 118 bottom. Daniel Bendjy: 107 top left. Grigory Bibikov: 97 bottom left. Maria Bibikova: 29 top left, 56 top left, 129 bottom right. Braddy: 113 top. Hilary Brody: 132 bottom left. Tony Campbell: 27 bottom center, 31 top left, 56 center, 65, 83 bottom, 109 top. catman73: 17 top left, 71 top. Yungshu Chao: 21 top left. Michael Chen: 19 top. Katerina Cherkashina: 23 top, 84 top (cat). Costin T: 60 bottom. Claudia Dewald: 60 top. DGID: 28 top left. Sharon Dominick: 143 both. dra_schwartz: 130. Lisa Eastman: 14. Irina Efremova: 99 bottom right. Sarah Fields: 26 bottom. Angus Forbes: 99 left. Daniel Gale: 71 bottom right. Eric Gevaert: 68 bottom. Globe Photo: 148 bottom left. Johanna Goodyear: 153 center left. Jerko Grubisic: 79. Memet Salih Guler: 92 bottom. Mark Hayes: 81 bottom. Joanne Harris/Daniel Bubnich: 107 top right. Mark Hayes: 146 bottom left. Barbara Henry: 53 bottom left. Stefan Hermans: 57 bottom, 95 top right, 114 bottom right. Ralf Hirsch: 41 bottom center. Eric Isselée: 17 bottom right, 21 top right. Jeff Jenson: 64. Joe_Potato: 31 bottom left, 137 bottom left, 148, 149 bottom right. Derek Jones: 59 bottom left. Sveta Kashkina: 15 top. Murat Giray Kaya: 82 bottom. Leslie Keating: 23 bottom left. Robert Kirk: 120. KMITU: 104 top. Jason Koenig: 106. Andrea Krause: 19 top. Simon Krzi: 78 center left. Zsolt Langviser: 123 top. Karin Lau: 55 top (cat). Kate Leigh: 27 right. Chiya Li: 74, 136. Avishay Lindenfeld: 121 top. Shannon Long: 134 bottom left. Martin Lovatt: 100. Susana Machado: 17 center left. Sue McDonald: 35. Denise McQuillen: 43. Tara Minchin: 22. Martina Misar: 126. Slobo Mitic: 95 top left. Kay Nieuwenhuis: 42 bottom left. Andrew Nokes: 77 top. Sandra O'Claire: 117. Jennifer Oehler: 71 center left. Jeff Oien: 52-3,

73 top, 96. Rafal Olkis: 75 top. pederk: 103 top left. Fielding Piepereit: 41 bottom left. Oleg Prikhodko: 15 bottom. Svetlana Prikhodko: 86 top right. Achim Prill: 81 top. Olaru Radian-Alexandru: 17 bottom left. Jon Rasmussen: 58. Ronen: 95 bottom. Robert Rushton: 30 center left. Pavel Sazonov: 122 top. Jon Schulte: 76, 127 bottom right. Maksim Shmeljov: 18 top left. Ekaterina Shvigert: 21 center left. Nico Smit: 18 right. Dwight Smith: 16. Vicki Stephenson: 49 bottom right. Andrey Stratilatov: 93 center. Marzanna Syncerz: 101 bottom. Thepropshoppe: 89 top. Willie B. Thomas: 45 top left. Lidija Tomic: 42 top left. Audrey Toutant: 114 center. Nikolai Tsvetkov: 21 center right. Tomasz Tulik: 53 bottom right. Emrah Turudu: 84 top (hand). Jan Tyler: 139 top left. Inge van de Meeberg: 37 top left. Alberto Perez Veiga: 89 bottom. Angelo Villaschi: 21 bottom left. Beverley Vycital: 34 center left. Walik: 70 top left. Dave White: 48. Frances Wicks: 36. Elena Zapassky: 115 bottom.

Merial Animal Health Ltd: 145 top, 145 center left.

Shutterstock Inc.:
Aceshot1: 115 top. AGphotographer: 75 center. Trevor Allen: 105 bottom. Anita: 49 bottom left. Ryan Arnaudin: 68 top. Avesun: 80 bottom left. Mark A. Bond: 151 bottom right. Tony Campbell: 31 bottom right, 97 top right, 122 center right. Sarah Cates: 102 top. Lars Christensen: 112 center left. Drilea Cristian: 99 center right, 153 bottom right. Ross Dailey: 46 top. Anna Dickie: 118 top. Diane N. Ennis: 59 bottom right. Stephen Finn: 78 top. Glen Gaffney: 87 center. Stefan Glebowski: 99 top. Johanna Goodyear: 85 top. Ramzi Hachicho: 102 bottom. Margo Harrison: 32. J. Helgason: 61 bottom left. Nicole Hrustyk: 69 bottom. Iofoto: 119 bottom left. Ovidiu Iordachi: 69 top. Eric Isselée: 85 bottom. Frenk and Danielle Kaufmann: 138 bottom. Clarence S. Lewis: 104 bottom. Hannu Liivaar: 119 bottom center. Polina Lobanova: 125 center. Matt: 55 top (case). Vladimir Melnik: 152. Michelle Milano: 20. Elicia Murdoch: 54 bottom. Antonio Jorge Nunes: 80 bottom right. ORKO: 111 left. Mark William Penny: 121 bottom. Perrush: 151 top. Pichugin Dmitry: 121 center. Plastique: 39. Robert Redelowski: 75 bottom. Robynrg: 62 top. Kristian Sekulic: 30 bottom. Olga Shelego: 113 bottom. Dwight Smith: 13. Gina Smith: 27 bottom left. Andrey Stratilatov: 63, 110. Suponev Vladimir Mihajlovich: 73 bottom. Magdalena Szachowska: 87 bottom. Jozsef Szasz-Fabian: 2 bottom left. Ferenc Szelepcsenyi: 54 top. Denis Tabler: 128 bottom left. Nikolay Titov: 111 bottom center. Simone van de Berg: 67. Zavodskov Anatoliy Nilolaevich: 150. Zoom Team: top left.